INSTANT SYSTEMS

Other Books in the Instant Success Series

Successful Franchising by Bradley J. Sugars

The Real Estate Coach by Bradley J. Sugars

Billionaire in Training by Bradley J. Sugars

Instant Cashflow by Bradley J. Sugars

Instant Sales by Bradley J. Sugars

Instant Leads by Bradley J. Sugars

Instant Profit by Bradley J. Sugars

Instant Promotions by Bradley J. Sugars

Instant Repeat Business by Bradley J. Sugars

Instant Team Building by Bradley J. Sugars

Instant Referrals by Bradley J. Sugars

Instant Advertising by Bradley J. Sugars

The Business Coach by Bradley J. Sugars

INSTANT SYSTEMS

BRADLEY J. SUGARS

New York   Chicago   San Francisco   Lisbon   London
Madrid   Mexico City   Milan   New Delhi   San Juan
Seoul   Singapore   Sydney   Toronto

5 6 7 8 9 0   DOC/DOC   0 9 8

ISBN 0-07-146670-3

This publication is designed to provide accurate and authoritative information in regard to the subject matter covered. It is sold with the understanding that neither the author nor the publisher is engaged in rendering legal, accounting, or other professional service. If legal advice or other expert assistance is required, the services of a competent professional person should be sought.
—From a Declaration of Principles jointly adopted by Committee of the American Bar Association and a Committee of Publishers.

McGraw-Hill books are available at special quantity discounts to use as premiums and sales promotions, or for use in corporate training programs. For more information, please write to the Director of Special Sales, McGraw-Hill Professional, Two Penn Plaza, New York, NY 10121-2298. Or contact your local bookstore.

Library of Congress Cataloging-in-Publication Data
Sugars, Bradley J.
Instant Systems / Bradley J. Sugars
p. cm.
ISBN 0-07-146670-3 (alk. paper)
1. Decision support systems.   I. Title.
HD30. 213.S84 2006
658.4'038011—dc22   2005025419

"It must be remembered that there is nothing more difficult to plan, more doubtful of success, nor more dangerous to manage, than the creation of a new system. For the initiator has the enmity of all who would profit by the preservation of the old institutions and merely lukewarm defenders in those who would gain by the new ones."

Machiavelli (1469–1527)

■ CONTENTS

■ INTRODUCTION

Systems: This has to be one of the most misunderstood areas of business today. I find this rather strange, because it's one area of business that's easy to implement, and one that will make your life, and those of your team members, so much easier. And it also happens to be something that will make your business run smoothly, efficiently, and profitably.

I'm big on systems for another very important reason: They allow your business to work *without* you.

That's right. They will allow you to live your dreams, to do the things you want to do, and to spend your time pursuing other, more lucrative goals like increasing your wealth.

I'm big on systems for another reason too. It all has to do with my basic philosophy of what business is all about. And it also happens to be what I am all about. Central to all this is, of course, the business, yours and mine. To understand what I mean you need to know what my definition of a business is. I define a *business* as a commercial, profitable enterprise that works *without* you.

Let that sink in for a moment.

I know it seems to be 180 degrees away from what you've been taught in the past. Think about it; why build a job for yourself when you can build an income stream that keeps on growing whether you're there or not? Remember this one simple fact: The only reason you would ever start a business is to sell it at some point in time. Your business is your product, it's what you're building, and it's where you're ultimately going to make your profit when you sell it.

Very few people ever make a fortune running their businesses, but a lot of people make a fortune selling them.

Look at Bill Gates, for instance. Sure, he's made a lot of money selling software, but he became the richest man in the world by selling shares in his business, Microsoft.

Are you too involved in your business? Could you pick up the phone in the morning and say to whomever answered, "You guys look after things. I'm taking three months off." If you are like the vast majority of business owners out there, you would very definitely answer *no*.

Why? Because your business wouldn't have the systems in place that would allow it to function effortlessly without you.

Let's look at it from another perspective. Perhaps you don't trust your team members to get on and do the job themselves. Perhaps you can't let go of running "your baby." Perhaps no one there can *do* the job as well as you can.

If this sounds familiar, ask yourself this: Why did you buy or start your business in the first place? Think hard now. And be honest with yourself. Did you not just buy yourself a job?

Understand that this is *not* what owning a business is all about. If you continue working *in* it and not *on* it, then your business will never grow and prosper, and it will not reach its full potential.

It's for this very reason that you have to get yourself out of the day-to-day routine of running the business. Stop working from nine till five, doing the work *of* your business. It's like the carpenters that don't run their businesses. Instead they spend all day using a hammer and nails, working *in* their businesses.

Imagine that when you started your business, you built it in your mind first, and then you drew a picture on paper of what it would be like when it was finished. That's right; you've got to finish a business at some stage and have it ready for sale.

As an example, imagine buying this book after I'd slapped together only an outline of each chapter and hadn't finished writing it. How much would you pay for it, only a fraction of its full price? The same applies in business. People try to sell a business that hasn't been finished, so they're really only selling a *job*. Of course, they'd get only a fraction of the price for it too.

When you've got the finished picture firmly in your mind, you then go to work creating that business. That means working *on* the business, rather than just working *in* it.

In fact, you're designing the business so it will run whether you're there or not. Then you've got choice, and choice to me equates to freedom. You can keep the business, or you can sell it. You can work in the business or you can spend your time more creatively.

Now, take a moment and imagine a business that you didn't have to work in. Would the business still *work*? I mean would it function properly? Would all the systems and people integrate to achieve the result you want and the result your customers want? *Of course it would.*

Almost all business owners I've ever met work so hard (too hard) for this exact reason. Their business doesn't work—they do. Everything about the business is in their heads, and they're the only people who can do anything, so they're trapped. Imagine my example of this book and how hard I'd have to work if this knowledge were only in my head.

Most owners are like this because they don't trust anyone else to do the job. For some reason they believe that no one else can do it as well as they can. They have to be in control.

All great leaders are good at delegating, so start off-loading some of your tasks *now*!

By the way, once you've given your team members the job to do, let them do it. Don't jump in to save them; that way they'll never learn how to get the job done. All they will learn is that you're the only one who can fix things, so you always will. Remember, sometimes you have to let them fall off the bike to learn how to stay on.

There's another reason I find doing business in this day and age interesting; it has to do with the *age* we're in. Let me explain. The nineteenth century was called the industrial age; the twentieth century was the so-called information age, and the latter part of the twentieth century became the age of knowledge. I believe the twenty-first century will become known as the lifestyle age or the edutainment age, but with the pace at which things happen these days, perhaps this will only last decades, and not a full century.

Now, what made the industrial age so exciting and successful was precisely the fact that industrialists developed a systems approach to their businesses. They had to introduce systems to cope with the speed with which their factories began producing products. But as time went on and they moved into the twentieth century, they didn't suddenly sweep out everything they had learned; they expanded on their information base by adapting what they had to what they were discovering. And so it was that newer, faster, and more efficient ways of manufacturing were invented. Henry Ford discovered that if he introduced a production line to his factory, he could produce cars even faster.

Industrialists knew the power of the systems approach and they made good use of it. Progress was happening at a phenomenal rate. Now, these systems were all predominantly factory or production based, but they were still systems. Then, as the twentieth century progressed, information became the major commodity with the development of the computer.

Computers are systematic things. They rely on systems to work. All that really happened was that computers had taken the place of machines, but the basic approach remained highly systemized.

The information age slowly gave way to a knowledge-based age, and now that we are firmly in the twenty-first century, we have been able to harness our knowledge and use it to give us the lifestyle we desire. When you come to think of it, knowledge is just a higher level of information, isn't it? Knowledge is all about what we do with information.

Knowledge also implies more of a human connection than does information, in which the machine has pride of place. Humans have now regained their rightful place at the top of the pile. And it's in the business and not the factory where the action takes place.

During the switch from factory to office, something was forgotten along the way. The office managers may have thought their factory floor counterparts were beneath them or something, because they certainly didn't take a leaf out of their books when it came to organizing and running their businesses. This distinction was further highlighted by the *white collar/blue collar* distinction.

The new breed of businessmen largely ignored the need to systemize their operations. Business owners seemed determined to *do it their way.*

Not all businesses blundered on blindly, however. The so-called big end of town certainly introduced systems, but largely out of necessity due to the size of its operations. It was all but impossible for one person, the owner or managing director, to do everything himself. Not so with small business.

Over the past few years my coaches and I have helped many hundreds of small businesses to introduce systems, and the results have been nothing short of stunning.

This book is all about systems and how you can introduce them into your business. The new knowledge you're about to learn could be the most powerful you've ever learned. It will transform your business, freeing you up so you can devote your time to other things, like being with your family, starting another business, or really looking for investment bargains in the real estate market.

So, congratulations on deciding to take proactive steps to growing your business. By concentrating on first things first, you'll set in motion a chain of activities that will ensure that your business runs smoothly without you. It will set your business up so that it runs entirely by systems, which in turn are run by your people. I personally guarantee it.

This book is designed to give you the inside track on everything you need to know about systematizing your business. It aims at providing you with an *instant* guide on how to identify which areas to systemize, how to develop and write the systems, and how to implement them without causing mass panic among the members of your team. It will show you how to slowly extricate yourself from the business, while ensuring those who take over the reins do so in a competent and responsible fashion.

This book is the next step in your success story. From this moment on, you won't have to dream about the day when you're recognized as a leader in your field. You'll know precisely what to do to make it a reality. You'll also wonder why you didn't do it sooner.

■ How to Use This Book

This book is divided into different parts, one for each of the major aspects that relate to systemizing a business. It takes a close look at how you go about identifying areas in your business to systemize, how to develop and write the systems, four key areas of your business to systemize, the nine steps you need to take when systemising your business, how to implement your systems without causing mass panic at work, and finally how to extricate yourself from the business.

Start at the beginning, jump right in, and begin working through the steps outlined. Each step covers an important aspect of the processes being discussed. You see, there are things that you must give careful consideration to before getting carried away doing the *fun* things involved in systemizing your business.

We'll begin by catching up with my mechanic Charlie, who decided it was time he began introducing systems to his business. Now those who know him will be aware that he's no business tycoon. He doesn't have a mind for business. But he soon realized the need for systems to run his business. Follow his experiences and learn as he did about the role systems can play in any business. You'll discover, like he did, the power systems can have on your business and how it can turn your future around.

You might also be surprised at how much this exercise will reveal about your business. It may get you thinking about important issues that have never crossed your mind before. If some of this information is new to you, don't be concerned. There's never been a better time to start working *on* your business.

Make sure you make notes as you go along. When you come to designing your own systems, you'll find it useful referring back to them. You'll find proven examples and ideas that, when combined with your new knowledge, will bring results.

Now it's time to get started. There are customers out there waiting to deal with you. All you need right now are the right systems to run your business, and the right people to run your systems. And where does that leave you? It leaves you free to do whatever you want to do.

So what are you waiting for? It's time to get into *Action*.

▌ Charlie Systemizes and Shifts to Top Gear

My relationship with Charlie, my trusted mechanic, goes back a long way. He had been recommended by a friend when I bought my first sports car nine years ago, and I've always been more than happy with the work he has done for me since.

He came highly recommended and I can see why; his work is second to none, his prices are competitive, and he gives great customer service. He really is more than just a mechanic—he's a car enthusiast as well.

But the more I got to know him, the more I realized that he knew very little about running a business. But to be fair to him, I'd have to say that he was no worse than most business owners I'd met. He knew how to do his job well. But this was where he was going wrong, because he actually owned the garage, he didn't just work there as one of the mechanics.

The more I had to do with the business, the more I could see that it wasn't reaching its full potential. In fact, it was nowhere near as successful as it should have been. You see, Charlie was spending all his time working *in* his business and not *on* it. Nobody was planning ahead, putting in place the building blocks that would take the business to the next level, and then the one after that.

But who could blame him? The system doesn't teach people how to successfully run a small business. Sure, it teaches them how to do various jobs well, but it doesn't teach them what really matters: The attitude needed to prosper, the real functions of a business owner and the strategies involved in working on the five key areas of any business, what I call the *Business Chassis*.

Then, as Charlie and I became friends, I began coaching him, and his eyes were opened! He told me that he had no idea how off the mark he had been, as far as running a business is concerned. We started slowly, working on the first part of the Business Chassis, the leads. Once he had begun receiving a steady flow of new leads, we turned our attention to the next part of the Business Chassis, his conversion rate. That was a real eye-opener. Charlie had no idea that he actually had to convert his prospects into customers. He simply assumed that it would just happen all by itself. He thought people who needed their cars serviced would become customers, if they thought his price was right. But I wasn't surprised. Most people seem to think the same way.

The next part of the Business Chassis that we worked on was the number of transactions his customers made. Jut a small 10 percent increase here made a *huge* difference to his business, and his profit. After that we tackled his average dollar sale. This is the fourth part of the Business Chassis. Charlie was able to identify missed opportunities and implemented strategies aimed at correcting this, and increasing the average amount his customers spent when having their cars serviced at the same time. Charlie was truly amazed by what these strategies did for his business.

The final part of the Business Chassis, the margins, was perhaps the most illuminating for Charlie. You see, we were able to try things his inner self said he shouldn't, like increasing his prices by 10 percent. He really didn't want to do this, but I insisted. He was stunned when all it did was give him more profit. He didn't lose a single customer. In fact, none of them even noticed!

After having worked on the Business Chassis, Charlie's Garage started to become well known in his area. His customers began noticing the difference, not only in their whole experience visiting the workshop, but also because they could feel that there was a buzz about the place. Charlie began extricating himself from the workshop and began to spend more time managing and directing. At first he felt strange in his new role, but after a while he began to really enjoy it. As he became comfortable working on the business, he began to become more adventurous. He also began thinking like a businessperson and not a mechanic.

The more Charlie began working *on* his business, the more potential he began to see. He started thinking more about growing the business than ever before, but the more involved he became with these plans, the more he realized he needed to devote his time to this aspect of the business. It was becoming abundantly clear to him that he really needed to hand over his responsibilities for the workshop to one of his team members, so he could get on and concentrate entirely on the future. But he was, quite naturally, scared of the consequences. He didn't want any setbacks and he was afraid things would go off the rails without his being there to keep an eye on things.

It was this that brought me to his office for another meeting.

"Good morning, Charlie, nice to see you again," I said as I stepped into his small, but functional office. It's funny how offices in mechanical workshops are all the same—cluttered with engine replacement parts and old furniture. It's no wonder most garage owners see themselves as desk-bound mechanics.

"Glad you could make it," he replied, pulling out a chair for me before seating himself at the other side of his chaotic desk.

"So tell me, Brad, what's your latest baby?"

We always talked cars before getting down to business.

"You aren't going to believe this Charlie, but I have on order a Mercedes-Benz SL55 AMG. It's one of only a handful in Australia."

"You've got to be kidding! I mean, that's the most awesome car, from what I've read. When will it be delivered?"

"I'm hoping early next week. The dealer tells me they are having some publicity photos taken while they have it. Then once they've done that, it's mine."

Charlie was sitting on the edge of his chair now and staring at me intently. He let out a long, slow whistle.

"Man, I can't believe it. Do you reckon I can get a look at it as soon as it arrives? I mean, I've read about it and I'm eager to have a look at its engine."

"No worries, Charlie. I'll drop by on my way home from the dealer. You'll not only be the first to see it, you'll also be the first to have a ride in it."

He sank back into his chair, looking satisfied. Then, after a short pause, he continued.

"Brad, the reason I've asked you to drop in is because I think the time is right for me to begin thinking about ways for me to start handing over responsibility for running the garage to Jim, my foreman. I think I need to free myself up so I can concentrate on issues that have now become really important to me, issues like ensuring the business can run itself smoothly while I concentrate on building up my own wealth. You know, I'd like to start investing in real estate, and from what you've told me, I need to spend time hunting for a few bargains with great potential as positive-geared investments."

This pleased me to no end, because I knew Charlie was now taking his business very seriously. He had been listening to what I had been telling him in all our coaching sessions.

"I'm very glad to hear it, Charlie. What we're going to talk about now are ways that you can ensure that you're business performs, just like you'd want it to, all day, every day, without things going drastically wrong. In fact, your business will begin to operate as smoothly as a purring engine, whether you come in or not. See, what we're going to do is put systems in place to run your business. And these systems will ensure that the job gets done perfectly every time, irrespective of whether members of your team leave, get sick, or take vacations."

"But, Brad, how will that work? I mean, surely my people are the important ones?"

"Sure they are, but for a different reason. You see, once we're through and you have a whole series of systems in place, it'll be the systems that run your business, and your people who will run the systems. That way personalities don't get involved, and if someone phones in sick, anyone else can do that person's work by just getting the operations manual out and following the step-by-step instructions. Things won't come to a standstill, and you won't have to fend off irate customers with excuses when their cars aren't ready when promised."

"Ah, so you're saying it's possible for us to build a business that runs like clockwork?"

"Yes I am, Charlie. And it's not difficult to do at all. It all comes down to putting systems in place. You see, systems aren't emotional, they don't call in sick, and they don't make mistakes. It's entirely possible that, along the way, circumstances or the business environment changes, making the systems not as well suited to your evolving business as before. Then all we need to do is change, update, or fine-tune the systems. That's the beauty of it."

I could tell he was really interested, but I didn't want to go too far ahead at this point. It was time to get down to basics.

"Charlie, I think we need to begin examining which areas of your business to systemize, and how to develop and write those systems. Shall we make a start?"

"Yes, Brad, let's go for it."

INSTANT SYSTEMS

$$\boxed{\textbf{Part 1}}$$

▌ How to Identify Areas to Systemize

Before you begin doing anything to your business, particularly if what you have in mind is going to have a profound effect on the business, it's vital that you begin with a very clear picture of the status quo before you start.

It's much like altering the settings of your computer. It's great fun trying various settings and preferences, but unless you know what you're doing, you could end up going along a course or in a direction you don't want. Things might not work out as you'd planned. So what do you do? Well, with computers, you have a fallback position. You can always revert to the default setting. You can switch everything back to how it was before you started tampering.

That's a great feature, I can tell you, because it's saved many people from absolute chaos.

The situation can be exactly the same in business. You can change things as much as you like, but unless you have a detailed idea of what your business was like before you started implementing changes, you can never revert to how it was before. That's largely because new strategies tend to take time to implement, test, measure, and evaluate. Members of your team subjected to those changes obviously get intimately involved with the new directions their jobs take, and after a while, will tend to forget exactly how they went about their tasks previously. They are usually unable to revert to their previous situation should they be asked to.

Don't rely on the members of your team to reset your business. It's not their job to do so and it's unfair asking them to. You are the responsible person, after all, so that task falls into your lap.

So, how would you go about it?

The very first thing you need to do is to establish your default position. You need to establish exactly what your business is like before you begin doing anything. You need, in effect, a snapshot of your organization as it is right now.

Draw an Organogram

This is how you can develop an organogram, or a chart of your organization:

- Start with the head of the business, which presumably is you. Put the name of your position down at the top of the chart and in the center. Draw a box around it. This is the top layer in your organization.

- Next write down the names of the positions that report to you. Draw a box around each of them and connect them to your box by means of straight lines. This is the second layer in your organization.

- Write down the names of all the positions that report to the positions that occupy the second layer. Draw boxes around them and connect them with straight lines, known as reporting lines, to their respective second-layer positions.

- Carry on in this fashion until you have your entire organization mapped out.

This is how it should look:

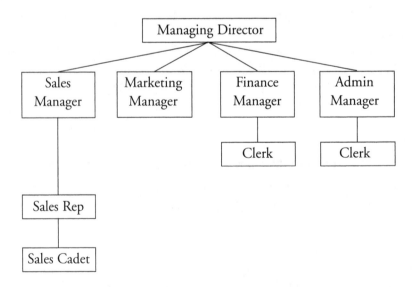

Develop Flowcharts

Now that you have drawn up an organizational chart of your business, the next thing you need to do is to develop a flowchart for each functional area or department in your business. This chart will describe in detail and with accuracy exactly what happens in each area. Think of it this way: It charts the path work takes through that department.

Here's what you do:

- Take one functional area at a time and work your way through it before tackling the next area, then the next, until they have all been documented.

- Start at the first point of contact with your customer for goods or service.

- Document the flow of the job as it passes through the functional area, from start to finish, or until it passes through to the next functional area.

- Draw boxes around each function, and then join them up with straight lines.

As an example, let's start with the sales function in the diagram below.

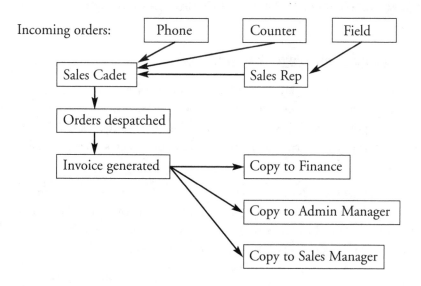

Bradley J. Sugars

Involve Your Entire Team

It is extremely important to explain to all team members exactly what you'll be doing, why, and what the expected outcome will be *before* you begin documenting or observing what they do. The last thing you want is for them to become suspicious—the grapevine will spring into action and your intentions could backfire badly. Explain that it's not a witch-hunt, that you're not looking for excuses to do away with them or their jobs, and that you're not aiming to consolidate various positions, making some of them redundant.

You really do need to ensure that you get all team members aboard for an exercise like this, as they can be of enormous assistance, and if you don't, you could end up with a big problem on your hands. So consult widely and honestly. Involve them in every step of the exercise. Communicate genuinely and hide nothing. Let them know what your intended outcome is: Making the business run smoother, more profitably and efficiently, with major benefits for them, their workload, and their level of job satisfaction.

Get this aspect right and it can turn into a major team-building exercise with huge benefits as far as team morale is concerned. If you involve all your team members from the very beginning, they will buy into and take ownership of the exercise. Your job will become very much easier, the end result will be much more effective, and the final outcome will exceed your wildest expectations.

Document What Each Team Member Does

Now that you know exactly how work flows through each of your functional areas, the next thing you need to understand, and document, is exactly what happens at each point as it makes its way through this area to the next. What we are interested in is exactly what each person working in this area does on a daily, weekly, and monthly basis.

This is a fairly detailed task and one that could take a fair amount of time to complete. But it is absolutely necessary that you don't cut corners, take shortcuts, or leave things out. The object here is to gain a clear and accurate picture of what happens in your organization. This has three main purposes:

- It provides you with your default position.

- It gives you accurate data from which to produce your system.

- It provides information to allow you to streamline the operation, making each position more efficient.

There are various methods you could use to achieve this. They include the following:

- Interview team members.

- Ask team members to write a detailed report of what they do.

- Observe team members.

- Video team members.

- Record on audiotape details of what the team members do.

Once you have produced a detailed description of what each and every team member does, tidy it up and edit the copy so that it reads well. Then get the team members concerned to review what you have written in order to give you their approval or suggest corrections so that the end result is an accurate reflection of what happens in their areas of responsibility *at that time.*

Remember, don't jump ahead here and start changing what they do because you have uncovered more efficient or cost-effective ways of doing things through this task audit. That's not the purpose. You see, you are interested in getting a detailed map of how things run in your business *at the moment.* You are busy compiling your default position that will allow you to instantly revert to the status quo if new methods or ways of doing things don't prove to be better than what was done before.

And you can't guess or assume anything here. Everything will be thoroughly tested and measured to ensure that it works as intended. But if it doesn't, then at least you have a safety measure up your sleeve.

Run through this exercise with everyone in that functional area or department, and then do the same for the next functional area, and then the next, until you have worked your way through your entire organization. Collate the documents together, and the end result is a detailed snapshot of what goes on workwise in your organization. You could think of it as a comprehensive operations manual. File it in a folder and put it to one side for the moment.

It is important to bear in mind that what you are aiming for is something quite different than a set of job descriptions or *Key Performance Indicators*. Resist the temptation to take a shortcut by simply using people's job descriptions. What people *actually* do in a job and what they are *supposed* to do is usually quite different. Furthermore, we are aiming at compiling a detailed account of what *happens* every day, week, or month, and not what *tasks* need to be looked after. Get the difference?

This is important because when it comes to writing the systems, you will be concerned with finding out what is working and what isn't in every job in your business. You will be looking for better, more efficient, and cost-effective ways of conducting your business, with benefits in everything from customer satisfaction to team satisfaction, and from increases in profit to a more efficient business operation. Job descriptions can't help you achieve this.

Part 2

■ How to Develop and Write the Systems

Once you have a complete and detailed description of what your team members do on a daily, weekly, and monthly basis, your next task will be to test and measure what they are doing to see if it is producing the required results.

Now's the time to compare these activity schedules with their respective job descriptions and Key Performance Indicators (KPIs). The aim here is not to catch people or to go about pushing them to work harder in a sneaky way; it's about finding better ways of doing things.

The Japanese have a great word for this. They call it *Kaizen,* and it means constant and never-ending improvement. Think of your quest for improvement as a circle; it has no beginning and no end. It is a never-ending quest. You just keep getting better all the time. When you have reached your goal as far as improvement is concerned, then raise the bar a little and try again. When you reach that level, raise the bar again and improve some more.

Test each job one at a time. Start by comparing what is actually done with the KPIs. Are the KPIs being achieved? Are they all being achieved on time, or only some of them? What are the reasons for this? Can steps be put in place to correct this?

Once you have ascertained how each job scored, you need to involve your team members. Get them to do the following:

- List their top 10 time-consuming tasks.

- List their top 10 stressful tasks.

- List their top 10 productivity-related tasks.

- List their top 10 tasks that bring them the most happiness.

Now, how can you accommodate the above four lists in their daily, weekly, or monthly routines? Can you streamline, adapt, amend, correct, or include something new here? Ask your team members to think about any bottlenecks they are aware of. Get them to list the three that they believe are causing the greatest problems to customers or to your bottom line. You'd be surprised what your team members actually know about your operation—they do, after all, work closely with it day in and day out. Work at eliminating these problems one at a time. Then have a look at making absolutely sure the team members' 40 points are taken into account. You see, not only will you be taking their concerns on board, you'll be seen as doing something positive to address some of the major job-related issues facing them. Having satisfied or content team members means that your business will operate more efficiently and cost-effectively. There will be a real sense of purpose and pride, and your customers will pick this up.

Now it's time to rewrite, with the assistance of each team member, the daily, weekly, and monthly task descriptions. Alter the job descriptions and KPIs accordingly. Monitor how they are performing and coping for a month, then test and measure the work descriptions against the KPIs once more. You should see a huge difference in performance levels, job satisfaction, and results.

If the new job functions are performing according to plan, then consolidate at this new level for the next 12 months. Let things settle so they become standard procedure.

Do the same for all the other positions in your organization, then bind all the resultant documents together, sorted by functional area or department, and the result will be a complete systems manual for your business.

So, how do you go about actually writing the systems manual? It's not as daunting as you'd imagine. Here are some considerations:

- Start with the work flow descriptions.

- Use bullet points and concise headings.

- Start with the first, or most important, or regular task.

- Itemize each action that is needed to handle or complete each function, and write briefly what needs to be done.

- Mention what the desired outcome is, and what happens next.

- Don't forget to mention what happens if things go wrong or if another action is called for.

As an example, let's refer back to our sales department and write up the system for handling telephone orders.

This is what it could look like:

Handling Incoming Telephone Orders

- When the telephone rings, the Sales Cadet will answer it after three rings.

- Say, "Good morning. Thanks for calling Mumbo Jumbo; this is James. How can I help you?"

- When the caller says that she wants to place an order, say, "Certainly; would you mind if I run through a couple of questions to ensure that I get the details of what you want to order?"

- Reading from the sales script, which is written on the sales order form, obtain details of the order, the delivery address, and the method of payment.

- Confirm the details with the customer by reading back the details to her.

- Thank the customer for the order and hang up.

- Make a copy of the completed order form.

- Send the original to the dispatch department and file the copy in your orders file.

- Write up a sales invoice, with three copies.

- E-mail one copy to Finance, one to the Admin Manager, and one to the Sales Manager.

Then do the same for each and every function within your organization, collate all the descriptions according to functional areas or department, file them, and produce a cover page with a suitable title, such as *Sales Department Systems.*

Part 3

∎ The Four Key Areas to Systemize

Now you have a basic set of systems in place and you're reasonably happy that they are working. The next step is concentrating on writing or developing systems that affect the business as a whole and will put your business well and truly on the fast track to operating smoothly and efficiently all day long.

We are no longer focusing on writing systems at the job level, but higher up at the corporate level. These will be company systems that will govern how the business in its entirety operates.

When viewing any business from a corporate perspective, there are four key areas that encompass every other system that you have in place. You see, there are some that will be common across the board, so rather than duplicating them over and over again for all your different functional areas, these systems are grouped together under the corporate portfolio.

So what are these four key areas of the business? They are:

1. People and Education.

2. Delivery and Distribution.

3. Testing and Measuring.

4. Systems and Technology.

By concentrating on writing systems for these broad areas, you'll be putting in place ways to make your business work more efficiently and effectively.

Let's look at them now one by one and in some detail.

People and Education

Ever heard of the saying, "People are a company's best asset?" I'm sure you have. And it's true. But when we're talking about systems for people, I believe we also need to include education. People need to have their skills updated from time to time to remain *relevant* to your business. Now I know this sounds a bit cold and impersonal and I don't mean it to, but the fact remains that people, like any other business tool, system, or asset, need updating or they'll *depreciate,* and that's something we don't want.

Looking after the well-being and welfare of your team members will not only make them feel relevant, wanted, and of value, it'll also help them feel competent and comfortable with their work. Content team members are productive team members, and this means a business that will function smoothly and profitably.

What systems could you implement to achieve this? Here are a lot for you to consider.

Run an Ongoing Training System

Keep your people growing and moving forward; it's the best way to ensure that they keep the company growing.

Your people really are your best asset. And here's another business truism: If you aren't going forward, you're going backwards. There is no middle ground. The same is true for people in this information age. It's all about knowledge. Empower the people who work for you with knowledge. It will pay you handsome dividends.

Don't worry that you might spend time and money training them to the point where they become attractive to your opposition. Sure, you might lose a few, but think of the consequences. I'd rather lose one or two people than my business, because that's what will happen if your team stagnates.

So how do you train them? And what type of training should they receive? Let's start with the first one. There are various types of training courses you could consider. These include:

- Induction training for new employees.

- On-the-job training, where an experienced employee trains a newer employee.

- Departmental training sessions, where groups receive formal training together.

- In-house training, where the trainer is a team member.

- External training sessions or courses, where team members are trained at external venues by external trainers.

- Specialist training, where external trainers are hired to train team members in-house.

- Private training, where team members are encouraged to attend private training courses and are then reimbursed by the company upon completion.

- Preretirement training, where team members are assisted in preparing for retirement.

The type of training you give depends largely on what type of business you run, but generally, there are some considerations that will guide you. These include:

- Technical training.

- Communication skills training.

- Supervisory skills training.

- Conflict resolution training.

- Computer skills training.

- Financial skills training.

- Management skills training.

- Telephone skills training.

- Sales skills training.

- First aid training.

- Emergency training.

Develop an Induction Training Program

Get people comfortable with the company as quickly as you can.

A good induction training program is also one of the first real interactions new employees have with the company, and it's a great opportunity to positively influence them early on. These programs can be used to continually motivate existing employees who will address the new employees, telling them about their experiences with the company and what their roles are.

What's more, a good induction training program portrays professionalism.

Run Team-Building Training Programs

The better people know each other, the more they'll do for each other.

Another great benefit of team-building training programs is that they get people together and focused. Once they've gone through the mill together, they will develop bonds and friendships that transcend those which can be developed in the normal office situation.

These programs can be run in-house with department heads or managers running the sessions. It's great training for them too, as they need to research and think deeply about their areas of speciality and how to teach them.

Complete Team Skill-Based Training Sessions

Group training sessions build team synergy and are effective in upgrading the skills of individual members. People learn better in groups, as they usually have different levels of knowledge and social skills. Individuals usually learn more from a group question-and-answer session than from studying at home at their own pace. The dynamics of group sessions are very powerful. They also do wonders for team building as well.

One of the primary reasons for organizing skill-based training sessions is the positive effect it has on team morale. Getting people to work as a team to achieve difficult tasks is a great way to achieve bonding. These sessions can be physical or mental. For instance, training sessions at paint ball combat courses, rock-climbing venues, and obstacle courses are a great test of endurance and ingenuity. Alternatively, group activities like quiz evenings or games nights also work well.

Complete Team Member Positional Contracts

If people are clear on what they're supposed to be doing, they will do a better job.

All team members are employed for a reason and have an important role to play. Let them know what that reason is, and the part they play in helping the business reach its goals.

A person's *positional contract* must clearly state the objectives, goals, responsibilities, and accountabilities of the position. It needs to state how the people doing the jobs will know when they have performed satisfactorily, when they have excelled, or when they have need to improve.

It also needs to state tasks to be performed, standards to be met, and goals to be achieved.

Have a Redundancy System

This way it's set up once and for all and applies to everyone.

Redundancy has to be one of the most contentious and potentially dangerous aspects of running a business today. Get it wrong and you could, at best, lose the support and trust of your team. At worst, you could lose everything in a long, drawn-out legal battle.

Because this is one issue that affects peoples' livelihoods, it is a very delicate matter. You need to ensure that you remain scrupulously clean in this regard. The best safeguard is to set up a system that is fair, honest, and transparent right from the start. There are a few systems you could adopt, such as last in first out, or those close to retirement age go first. Of course, you need to state what that age will be. You could also adopt a redundancy system that is based on performance. If employees perform below a certain predetermined level, or bring in less than a certain level of business, they would be considered first if redundancy were necessary.

Develop a Team Social Club

Get people playing together and you'll be amazed at how much better they work together.

The old saying, "All work and no play makes Jack a dull boy," is as true today as it ever was. By showing your team that you care for their social needs, as well as their professional ones, you will be making an investment in their well-being that will far outweigh the cost.

The social club is a place where team members get to really know each other as people, irrespective of their standing in the business. It's also a place where they can destress and chill out when the need arises. It's their territory and their safe haven.

You can go about developing a social club in a number of ways:

- You could get your employees to vote for a social committee, who will then be tasked to establish the club, which could either be funded by the business or by the employees via a monthly fee that is deducted from their salaries.

- You could establish the club yourself and run it like you would another department. In this case, it would be totally company funded.

- You could encourage your employees to join an external club, with the joining and membership fees being paid by the company on their behalf.

- A committee composed of members of management as well as employees could run the club.

Subscribe to Educational Newsletters, Magazines, Etc.

The more you and your team learn, the easier your jobs will become.

In today's fast-paced world, information is the key to success. It's also the key to allowing your business to stay ahead of its competitors. By subscribing to trade journals or newsletters that focus on your particular industry, your team members will be able to stay up-to-date and well informed on matters affecting their industry. They will feel more professional, especially when dealing with customers.

You could set up a library in your break room, kitchen, or social club room, or you could establish a magazine circulation list so these publications circulate to relevant team members. The drawback of the latter system is that magazines can take a long time to reach those at the bottom of the list.

Making newsletters and magazines available to your employees is a small investment that will pay huge dividends.

Develop a System for Conflict Resolution

It's going to happen whether you like it or not, so make sure your people know how to handle it when it does.

People are all individuals with different personalities, beliefs, and outlooks. They also have different expectations and levels of tolerance.

Stress is a fact of modern life, and so is competition. In the work situation, this results in conflict. Establish a system and the rules for conflict resolution early on. And make them available to everyone.

Your system should involve a mediator, who could be someone from your HR department or an external consultant. There are many specialist psychology firms that provide mediation services to business. Find them in the Yellow Pages or by phoning your local hospital or information hot line. And always allow the parties to nominate an advisor of their choice to assist them. This person could be a friend, a coworker, or a relative.

Develop Your Company's Rules of the Game

How should people act in your business, what are your standards, and how does everything work? Write them down and distribute them to your team.

Employees need to know what the boundaries are. They need to know what is acceptable and what is not. What dress code do they need to adhere to? What are the working hours and what happens during lunch hours? Are private telephone calls allowed and who can use the company car? You also need to address issues like overtime, going beyond the call of duty, and how to handle family matters. Certain antisocial matters can be addressed here too, like smoking in the work place and gossiping. But make certain that there is only *one* set of rules for the whole company; don't have a set for the employees and another for management. And don't allow the rules to be continually broken; otherwise people will soon lose faith in them.

Display the rules in all work places, public and staff areas, and in the canteen or social club.

It is a good idea to run through the rules with prospective employees when they attend employment interviews. They should be discussed and explained during induction training and at other convenient times. Remember, a good set of working rules will mirror or direct your company's culture.

Complete a Consistent Recruitment System

This way either you or your team can recruit people time after time.

One of the inherent dangers involved with recruiting new people is that you can get it wrong. You can appoint a square peg for a round hole. Many applicants can submit first-class resumes that paint a rosy picture. Many of these will have been professionally constructed with the primary aim of landing the job. Can you tell which are genuine and which are not? Appointing the wrong candidate can prove a costly mistake.

Develop a consistent recruitment system that takes the guesswork or gut feeling out of your selection process. Take into account all the elements that make a good team member: body, mind, heart, and spirit. Don't make the mistake of concentrating on body and mind only, as most employers do. Be sure to consider whether the applicants have the *heart* for the job. What passions do they have? What about enthusiasm and motivation? These factors are usually far more important than *mind* aspects such as knowledge, skills, and experience.

Develop a consistent system that is designed to test all the elements that make a good employee. Decide on how the selection process will operate and stick to it. Involve all your team members in the selection process—after all, they have to live with the chosen applicant.

Decide too how you go about sourcing suitable candidates for interviews. Will you entrust this function to an employment agency or will you advertise yourself? If you get a huge response do you have the time and manpower to sift through all the applications?

You also need to decide how you will structure your interviewing process. Will it be a group interview whereby 10 or 15 of the best applicants are interviewed simultaneously, or will you be interviewing applicants individually? Also, who will be conducting the interviews? Yourself as the owner of the business or will you appoint a responsible supervisor? What procedure will be followed? Will there be aptitude tests, or will your selection be based on personality, passion, and enthusiasm? What weighting will you place on references? Are they even worth contacting? These are some of the questions that you will need to resolve when developing your recruitment system.

Develop Contingency Staffing Plans

This is particularly important for key senior players. Make sure you train an understudy as soon as possible.

Everyone gets sick, takes leave, and has days away from the office for business or emergency reasons. Will this present you with a problem? Who will answer the phones if your receptionist calls in sick? And who will sign the checks if the general manager is out of town?

You need to develop contingency plans as part of your staffing system. Start with the position statements for each and every position in your company. Write down and get clear on who does what whenever someone is away from the office. This could follow lines of delegation or seniority within each department or functional area, or it could follow lines of reporting relationships.

Another great system worth considering is one that involves the rotation of positions. Let your team members switch responsibilities with others every few months. This will not only give them a greater appreciation of the role others play in the organization, it will also broaden their experience and provide you with a sound staffing contingency plan at the same time.

If your business has branches in different locations, swap team members between branches on a rotational basis. Also let people swap between different functional areas; why not allow a salesperson to spend six weeks working in the finance office while the finance controller gets to spend time out on the road?

Hold Regular Team Meetings

Communication is imperative if you're going to have a high-performance team.

Communication is the lifeblood of a business. Your people need to be kept informed. They need to be kept fully aware of matters that affect their immediate work area or function. They also need to know what future plans there are that will affect them.

This has two main advantages:

1. It helps them do their jobs better. They will know how to respond to customers if they get asked certain questions, and they will be able to portray a professional image. It will assist them in handling queries or requests from others, even though it may not be their specific function to do so.

2. It will also help build team spirit, as they will feel included. They will feel like true members of the team.

Bear in mind that most people hate attending meetings. One reason for this is because they are too long and can be counterproductive. If this applies to your business, then consider introducing rules aimed at ensuring that this doesn't happen at your business. Make all meetings last no more than 15 minutes. Have everyone attending stand during the meeting. That way you can be sure it won't run on for hours. Switch the chairperson or convenor on a meeting-by-meeting basis. And forget about having someone produce a formal set of notes. Keep it simple and informal.

You could run regular meetings at set times, like first thing Monday mornings and last thing on Friday afternoons. That way it's part of your routine and everyone knows they need to attend. But keep them meaningful, and short and sweet.

Develop a System for Recognition and Remuneration

Make sure your people know that they're valuable. Make sure that they always have something to strive for.

If people have goals to aim for, and if they know they will receive recognition for achieving them, they will give their best. Competition is a wonderful motivator. Yet in business, it needn't be competition against fellow team members. It could be competition against an individual's previous performance levels that motivate her.

Your system needs to be fair and consistent, or it could backfire. It should be linked with Key Performance Indicators and be taken into account when considering promotions and salary or wage increases.

Consider having regular prizes or awards for the most consistent performance, the most helpful team member, or the best performance of the week. Recognition can be made during your weekly meeting. Make a habit of acknowledging good work by commenting on people's achievements or efforts. Movie tickets for two are cheap, yet as a token of appreciation they are priceless. What can you do to encourage your employees to greater performances?

Some very successful businesses even award good performers with a stake in the company. Now that's an incentive that ensures the company continues to make as much profit as possible because dividends depend on it.

Use Behavioral, Personality, and Communication Analysis with All Team Members

This way they'll understand themselves, and you'll also know what position suits them best.

People change over time. Their skill level, their interests, and their desires change as they develop professionally and personally. Make sure that this doesn't work against the best interests of your business. Harness these changes for your mutual benefit.

By understanding these natural changes, you can inject fresh enthusiasm into a team member's career path. You'll also show your people that you have their best interests at heart.

Now I'm going to introduce you to two interesting concepts: NLP and DISC. By introducing them to the members of your team, you will give them an insight into why people do the things they do, how different people communicate with each other, and how to appreciate the differences between us.

Neuro-Linguistic Programming

NLP is a model of human behaviour and communication that draws from the knowledge of psychodynamics and behavioral theories. It is concerned with the identification of both conscious and unconscious patterns in communication and behavior and how they interact in the process of change.

So what does this mean as far as your team members are concerned?

If we can understand the three key components of NLP, we can become better communicators. These are:

- Rapport and communication.

- Gathering information.

- Change strategies and interventions.

Rapport and communication covers areas such as language-representational systems, eye-accessing movements, verbal and nonverbal pacing and leading, communication translation skills, and representational system overlapping.

Understanding NLP allows us to understand the processes people use to encode and transfer their experience and to guide and modify their behavior. The information gathering we do is done through three sensory systems: the visual, the auditory, and kinesthetic (feeling and touching). And to a lesser extent, we also use our senses of smell and taste. The really interesting thing here is that visual accounts for 40 percent of the way we communicate, auditory only 20 percent and kinesthetic 40 percent. Isn't that interesting?

So, what does this mean for members of your team? Well, one of the big lessons here is to learn to match the language system used by others when communicating with them. That way you build rapport really quickly. But be careful not to mimic their language, rather match and mirror the way they communicate.

Successful leaders also understand the various behavioral styles people have. They understand that people fall into one of four main behavioral groups. They can be either outgoing in nature, or reserved. Or they can be either task oriented or people oriented.

The DISC Personality Profile

It would help if we were able to understand, in broad terms, the way people behave. Understanding this would make our lives very much easier when it comes to interacting with them.

One system I recommend is the DISC Personality Profile. The American Psychologist Dr. William Moulton Marsden designed this system back in the 1920s. It places people into one of four different personality types, or categories: D—Dominant, I—Influential, S—Steady and C—Compliant.

The DISC Personality Profile is an accurate personality analysis that can be used to predict the behavior of individuals when they work on their own and with others. However, this system is not infallible. Like anything, it has its limitations. Its shortfall is that people seldom have just one personality. They are, rather, a combination of the four, just in different ratios. Everyone is dominant in one personality type, but another may be closely following.

The DISC test highlights a person's relative strengths in each of the four areas. The area that scores highest will be the person's dominant trait.

The results aren't always accurate, especially when the people being tested are aware of their personality eccentricities and have moved to improve these traits. The higher the strength shown from the test, the more the descriptions will fit. Don't use this as a definitive method for labeling peoples' traits. Use it as a guide to communicating with them. Part 6 deals with this in more detail.

Set the Company Vision and Write Your Mission Statement

Get your team members involved in where you're going and give them something to take ownership of.

Your people need to know where the company is heading if they are to help you get there.

You've got to build a *vision* of a big business, a business that needs to be big to achieve the vision you set. Maybe your vision is to change the world, to change your industry, or to be the best in your industry. Whatever your vision, the bigger it is, the bigger your business needs to become to complete it. Set a vision of what your business will be like when you've finished building it.

Your *mission statement* will tell your people what the company's most important ideals are. It will tell them how the vision is going to be achieved.

Once you and your team have decided on a vision and a mission statement, have them printed and framed. Display them in prominent areas of your business like the reception area, where your team members and customers can see them.

Your vision and mission statement are things to be proud of. They are also major focal points of your business that your team should be proud of and identify with. Show them off and use them as guiding lights.

Build Career Planning within the Company

Make sure your people can see where they're going and how they can grow within the company.

Well-defined career paths have the effect of reducing staff turnover. They also promote well-being, morale, and loyalty. Think of a career path as part of team members' development within the company. Their levels of knowledge, skills, and value are dramatically increased as they progress up the ladder.

You need to understand that if your people can see a definite, well-defined career path that excites them, they will become ambitious and work to progress within your organization. They will develop loyalty, which will in itself produce higher levels of efficiency and productivity. Pride in what they do will rub off on other, newer team members, who will pick up on the positive, vibrant atmosphere within the business. They will see firsthand that hard work and going the extra mile pay off. They will see that people do get promoted and progress within the business.

What types of career planning could you incorporate? Well, this very much depends on your business, but in general terms, there are a few options:

- Career progression within the team member's professional discipline.

- Career progression within the team member's department or functional area.

- Career progression into other functional areas of the business.

- Career progression into middle-management and senior-management levels.

- Career progression into affiliated or associated companies.

Set Company and Individual Team Member Goals

Give people direction, focus, and a sense of achievement.

Make sure the goals you set are achievable and realistic. Also be sure to distinguish between short- and long-term goals. Let people know how they reach their goals, what measures will be used to gauge whether they have succeeded or failed, and how they will know when they have reached their goals. Also let them know how the attainment of the goals helps the company reach its overall vision.

Make these goals meaningful, and the attainment of them in the interest of your team members. Link their individual goals to their Key Performance Indicators, and tie monetary bonuses to them. This way, when they achieve their KPIs, they receive a bonus on payday. But the bonuses you offer don't have to be monetary. You could offer days off, product, vacations, or anything else that would be viewed as worthwhile by your employees.

Consider having a chart that shows how your team members are tracking in the attainment of their goals. This introduces an element of competition and makes striving for goals fun. It can work particularly well in a sales environment, where salespeople can view how many sales they've made for the month by checking the sales chart. It also allows them to see how they are performing relative to the other salespeople.

Run Time Management Training

People can double their output with only a little more input if they know how to manage their time.

Time is a scarce resource. It's also nonrenewable. A little effort in time management can increase productivity enormously. This in turn will have positive benefits for people at all levels in the organization, as they will be able to meet their own goals and objectives more easily. It will help them perform better, meet their Key Performance Indicators, and be in the running for promotions or pay increases.

Consider running an in-house course on time management, with people from various functional areas attending. It will not only upgrade their skills, but it will also aid in bringing different team members together and so increase morale. Structure the content so that it benefits people's private lives as well. Provide useful take-home material that may assist with their children's homework or exam schedule. Consider hiring a well-known external facilitator to run the course.

You need to ensure that your motives aren't misinterpreted, though. You don't want your team members to think you're hell-bent on stamping out any idle time they might have just to increase your profit. Make sure they understand exactly what your aims are and why time management is important to them, as well as to the company. Link it to the achievement of KPIs and bonuses, for instance. And make sure you do allow them time to destress or chill out when needed. Perhaps you could introduce a new *chill-out* room, with plenty of reading matter, fresh tea and coffee, a fridge and microwave oven, and whatever else you feel necessary. Remember to include your team members when designing these areas, as having them involved will pay huge dividends.

Complete Positional *How-to* Manuals

This has been covered earlier in this book, but for the sake of completeness, I'll run through the major points again here. Don't just rely on the people you've got now; some of them will eventually move on. Write down how everything's done, so you can easily train the next person.

Not only will this give your people a sense of security knowing exactly what is required of them and how they must go about performing their tasks, it will also save time, money, and effort in the long run. The manuals will also prove beneficial when it comes to upgrading positions due to the introduction of new technology or the development of better processes.

Writing each manual is like doing an audit of each position. It will uncover any inefficiency that might exist.

Team Development

Your team can make or break your business. Develop the right environment and nurture your people through the development of effective and farsighted staffing plans and systems.

Set up mechanisms to foster team spirit and a culture that will promote the values as set out in your mission statement. Establish weekly team meetings, weekly management meetings, and regular *wifle* sessions (*What I Feel Like Expressing*) in which team members have uninterrupted time to speak their thoughts without fear of recrimination. Consider holding team-building weekends and rewarding exceptional contributions with awards or gifts. You could set up a team book, video, and tape library, and consider sponsoring a scholarship or apprenticeship. Mentor and buddy programs are extremely effective, as is getting the entire team involved with the selection of new team members. You could ask team members to suggest seven solutions to everyday workplace problems as part of a challenge, and invite them to celebrate their wins as part of the business culture. You could also allow them to participate in the ownership of any intellectual property they may develop. Royalty payments received when selling these patents or licensing them out would be regarded as a very substantial benefit. This could lead to passion in the team environment. The team could also be encouraged to perform community service programs after hours. You should also make it clear that you would be available to help any team member personally should the need arise.

Consider making your workplace family friendly by accommodating women with small children, allowing men to take maternity leave, or to have special family time at home should they need it.

Celebrate successes by holding a small function, announcing achievements to the whole organization, and giving awards or tokens of appreciation. Show the team members that they matter and that their development is in the overall interest of the business.

Delivery and Distribution

This is an area within any business that lends itself perfectly to systemization. It's the area that was originally mechanised and computerized when computers made their presence felt in the early days. Delivery schedules, production schedules, and stock prediction and forecast programs seemed perfect for computerization.

But systemization goes further than that, even in this functional area. Push the boundaries and notice a huge improvement in your business. Systemize whatever you can here and you'll be freeing up your resources for use elsewhere.

So what can be systemized in this area? Here are some suggestions:

Run Paperless Systems

If you can run your business via the computer and can avoid handling documents in triplicate, you'll save a mountain of time.

You'll also save heaps of money. Paper is expensive, and so is storage space. Massive filing systems are difficult to manage and to find documents in. They also need to be catalogued and expanded each year. Then there's archiving to be done every five years or so.

Electronic systems are easy to set up and manage. Data needs to be backed up regularly and stored off site. Specialist firms can take care of this function cost-effectively and without fuss. Or you can do it yourself.

One of the strengths of any computer system is the speed at which it processes information. So use it. Let it take over all the routine, mind-numbing tasks every business has. That not only frees up someone's time, it'll also do it more efficiently and a whole lot more quickly. Why store all that paperwork for years on end if you don't need to? The paperless system is a real possibility these days.

Deliver Your Service with Systematic Consistency

If there's a way to make great service happen time after time, then make sure your people are using it.

It's no use having a great system if nobody uses it, or only use it from time to time. The key to developing loyal customers through service delivery is to be consistent. It doesn't matter at what level you deliver the service; it has to be consistent to make an impression.

People like to know what to expect. They find comfort in the familiar. So give it to them.

That's one of the advantages of having systems that run your operation. That's right. They provide consistency and make sure things run smoothly.

Consistency also takes the guessing out of running a business. You'll know what's going to happen, when, and how. You don't need to ensure that you're always there, just in case something goes wrong. You can allow your energy, and that of others, to be directed towards other, more productive and profitable, areas.

Remember, consistency is the basis of good customer service, and good customer service is something most customers are willing to pay for. Remember too that providing great customer service without it contributing anything to your bottom line is a waste of time and money. It must contribute to the profitability of your business.

It all starts with consistency.

Change Product Packaging for Safer Delivery

If your deliveries are being returned because items are being broken in transit, then maybe it'll cost less to design new, safer packages.

First, have a look at what is happening in your distribution department. Perhaps all that is required is a change in the way your products are wrapped or prepared for delivery. Are they packaged in safe, sturdy, or impact-absorbing material? Are they wrapped in bubble wrap prior to being boxed or put into delivery envelopes? Are they being handled carefully at your end and do the packages carry the correct labeling? Designing new product packaging can be an expensive exercise, so speak to your delivery company first to find out how breakages can be minimized. There could be a cheaper solution, so look for this first.

If you have a delivery and distribution system, it is worth looking closely at how it functions. Perhaps it needs reviewing. Don't overlook asking those intimately involved with packing and delivering the product what might be done to overcome the problem. As they are closely involved, they might be able to identify problems and suggest solutions. If they can, be sure to give them the credit they deserve. It will work wonders for your team's morale and help raise productivity and efficiency.

If you decide to repackage, it can provide an opportunity to relaunch a product or to reposition it. This could justify an increase in price.

Either way, repackaging could increase your bottom line.

Reorganize Stock According to Highest Turnover

Make it easy on yourself. Everything that sells a lot should be easy to get to.

Think of rearranging your storeroom or warehouse. It will be easier to manage and will act as a visible sales barometer by allowing your team to see how fast the stock is moving. This in itself will help spur them on, as they will have a way of actually seeing how they are performing.

Place slow-moving stock items up high on shelves or low down on the bottom shelf. Make sure forklift trucks can get to fast-moving items easily. Also stock popular items closer to your loading bay so that double handling is avoided. This cuts down on the number of team members needed to handle stock, as well as minimizing breakages due to mishandling.

If slow-moving items are stored in a distinct place, their lack of movement might also become more noticeable, causing sales staff to make a conscious effort to sell them, even if this means at a discount. So pay careful attention to how you stock or store your product. You could arrange it so it works to your advantage.

Simplify Your Order Pick-and-Pack Process

If it's less time-consuming to put away and then distribute stock, you'll save a bundle.

The name of the game is to avoid duplication of effort. Labor costs are time-related, so draw up a flow chart of your distribution process to see if you can save time by simplifying your systems.

How many hands does each order have to pass through, from the time it is placed right up until it is dispatched to the customer? Is the invoicing handled separately or does the person who packs the order produce all the paperwork, including the invoice? Is it possible to automate the process as much as possible? If another firm manufactures it, can it be delivered directly without having to first pass through your warehouse? What are the implications of amalgamating your orders and distribution departments? Do you use a *just-in-time* stock ordering system?

Forecast Stock Movements

If you can accurately forecast how much stock you'll move by when, you'll always know what to order, when to order it, and what money you'll have to spend.

Inventory control is all about timing and knowing your business. Running out of stock can cost your business in lost sales. It can also cost you a customer. Conversely, having too much stock ties up capital unnecessarily. By having a good record-keeping system, you will be able to forecast stock movement so you can place replenishment orders in time to ensure optimum use of capital and maintain sufficient levels of stock.

This can be a very precise business, so utilizing a good computer system is the perfect option. However, you don't need to run a sophisticated stock control system to achieve results; it all comes down to communication. You need to establish good communication channels with your salespeople, who will have historical and season sales trends, expected sales forecasts, and likely forecasts at their fingertips. They will know what business they've tendered for and how likely they are to be awarded the business. They should also know of any surges in demand or anticipated slumps. Talk with your financial controller, because it's no use placing a large order at short notice only to be told there's a cashflow problem.

Get your internal communications right, apply what you learn to your inventory control system, and you'll find yourself operating very much more efficiently. You'll notice the results on your bottom line.

Complete a Purchasing and Stock-Receiving System

Make sure you only order what's needed. Why hold loads of stock just so you can supply any unusual demand, should it materialize? Also make sure you pay a good price for the stock you buy—why give money away? You must make a habit of insisting on a discount whenever you can. And don't forget to regularly check other suppliers to see if they can offer better prices than you currently enjoy. It's a competitive world and someone is always looking for new business. Finally, make sure you get what you've paid for. It's not uncommon for product to be short when delivered. Mistakes happen, but if you don't have a system in place to check, you wouldn't even know that you were missing items.

If you make your purchases and receive stock in a haphazard fashion, chances are some orders will cost you more than they should. Develop a system to ensure uniformity based on carefully considered guidelines. That way there will be less chance for human error or impulse buying costing you money. A good stock-receiving system will also ensure that mistakes made by your suppliers are picked up before the items are booked into stock. This will save you the added expense of retrieving these items and returning them for refunds or replacement, as well as the consequent losses that could be incurred through not having the item available for sale when needed.

There's no excuse for running out of stock, but there's little justification for holding excessive stock either.

Outsource Logistics and Warehouse Support

Specialist companies are often much better than you are at warehousing and distribution.

They have the expertise and experience and can deliver far cheaper services than you could by doing it in-house. This option allows you to concentrate on your core competencies by freeing up capital that could be diverted into other areas of your business. Warehouses, storerooms, forklift trucks, and dedicated logistics and warehouse personnel are all expensive. Can you do without the hassles and save by outsourcing?

By not having to worry about warehousing, you might be able to downsize and move into cheaper, more convenient premises. This is a trend that even the very largest of businesses are moving towards these days, and for good reason. Should you be looking into this?

Outsource All Delivery of Purchases

If you currently do all your own deliveries, stop paying for delivery vans and things you don't need. Have a specialist company handle it for you instead.

Transport is one of the single most expensive items for any company when you take into account the cost of purchasing and running a delivery fleet. Fuel, tires, servicing, and insurance might cost more than they're worth to you. Check your options and call for quotes. You may be surprised at how much you stand to save.

Specialist delivery firms are able to tell you exactly where any delivery is at any particular moment. They have sophisticated tracking facilities that enable you to respond to customer queries quickly and accurately. They'll love you for it.

Complete Regular Stock Takes

Make sure you know what you've got and be sure to use that information wisely.

If you don't know what you've got in stock at any particular time, then how do you know what profit you're making? Remember, *profit is king*. Managing your cashflow is the name of the game. Having cash tied up in stock that you don't know about is costly.

This also affects your stock-ordering system, the cost of storage, and whether you have shrinkage or not. You could also be incurring unnecessary losses through product passing its use-by date.

By knowing precisely what stock you have on hand at any particular time, you can use this information sensibly with your salespeople, initiating sales drives, discounts, or promotions. Seasonal items can be moved in time, use-by dates adhered to, and inventory levels kept under control. This will also have important implications on the financial side of the business, with a greater level of control being possible on monetary reserves.

Quantify Service or Product Delivery Costs

Know how much you're spending so you can look for ways to improve and systemize. Do you have these figures at your fingertips? Not many businesses do.

By conducting an in-depth study into the actual delivery cost to your business, you can weigh whether the cost is justified. By putting these costs under the spotlight, you may very well streamline your system by cutting out duplications and inefficiencies. At the very least, you will come up with a more efficient system that is cost-effective. You may decide that the best option is to outsource. Either way, you will now have a far better understanding, and control, of these costs.

Measure Quality and Professionalism of Service Delivery

The more you measure it, the better it gets. It's a simple step.

How many business owners actually measure this? They may measure the cost of delivery and build that into their mix, but what about measuring quality and professionalism? Remember, people are usually willing to pay for a superior service, so give it to them.

By keeping the quality of your service delivery operation under the spotlight, you're sure to improve its level of professionalism. But you need to ensure that you have a good measurement system in place. By constantly measuring quality and professionalism, you would also be constantly improving your delivery system, which in turn will improve the performance of the relevant team members. Their professionalism will increase, their jobs will get easier, and they will perform better.

Another aspect worth bearing in mind is that people usually prefer working for a professional organization, because they want to be involved with a winner. It's not only good for their morale; it's also good for their careers.

Follow Up and Measure Quality and Time of Delivery

Your customers love deliveries of a high quality delivered on time, so make sure they're getting them.

The proof of the pudding is in the eating. When it comes to business, the quality of your delivery service can make or break you. It's no use delivering an item that is damaged on route to your customer. It's also no good delivering a purchase later than when it was promised or needed.

By taking some simple steps to ensure that this aspect of a customer's interaction with your business is not found wanting, you will be going a long way to ensuring repeat business.

How about conducting regular surveys to find out just what your customers think about your service? Ask them what you can do to improve your level of service to them. Find out how your delivery service stacks up when compared to those of their other suppliers. Benchmark your delivery service and set goals for improvement. Let them know you are looking at ways to constantly improve.

Measurement Systems for Freight, Couriers, and Vehicles

Getting it there the first time, on time, saves everyone a lot of time and money.

This is one area that lends itself to systemization. Many good transportation systems exist, so if you can't develop your own, then buy one. Monitoring the effectiveness of your current system, be it formal or informal, will highlight areas for improvement. It may even indicate that outsourcing would be more efficient and cost-effective.

Going through this exercise will save you money and ensure that your customers remain happy with your service. It will also go a long way to ensuring that they do business with you again.

Measure and Use Reorder Levels

Never order before you have to and never run out of stock. This may sound obvious, but ordering before you have to not only ties up capital in unnecessary stock and storage space, it also uses limited cash resources.

You need to monitor stock movements to time reorders so they arrive just on time. Conversely, you must ensure that you never run out of stock, because this could not only cost you a sale, it could cost you a customer for good. You see, those customers might be forced to buy from your competitor because they may not be able to wait until your stock arrives. Then they find that they are happy with the new product and service, strike up a relationship, and stay. Your competitor would gain new customers by default after you had done all the hard and expensive work finding them and educating them. Remember, new customers need to buy from you at least two and a half times before they become profitable, because their initial purchases will be used to offset marketing costs that brought them to you in the first place. So why hand the advantage to your opposition by doing all the costly work involved in *buying* the customer for them?

Use an Order-Tracking System

Make sure every order is traceable, and then if anything disappears you can start tracking it down.

Things do go wrong from time-to-time, and deliveries do go astray. Losing a delivery may not seem like such a big deal on its own, but understanding the cause can help you ensure that it doesn't happen again. It could help tighten up or fine-tune your delivery system.

If an order does get lost, and your client finds that you instituted an efficient recovery or tracking system, any potentially damaging consequences could be turned into positive outcomes. You could salvage a good customer and the deal.

Roster Staff for Service Delivery

Know your busy times and roster your team accordingly.

There's nothing worse, from a customer's point of view, than having to line up at the checkout counter when there are several unmanned checkouts. Rerostering staff to speed up service delivery during busy times is far easier and less costly than having to cope with inefficiencies. It could cost you more than sales; it could cost you customers.

Conversely, why have staff manning idle checkout counters when they could be doing something more productive? Encourage multitasking. To optimize this system all you need to do is know when your busy times are and plan accordingly.

Increase Security

Stock damage and loss is never a major focus of any business (unless you happen to be in the security industry, of course) but you've got to make sure it's not happening at your business.

Stock shrinkage, pilfering, and theft are avoidable. They're an unnecessary factor that can too easily get out of hand if left unchecked. Increased security can also have the added benefit of increasing staff morale and customer satisfaction. It might be the smartest investment you make.

Increasing security doesn't only mean hiring security guards to patrol your premises. You could drastically improve your losses simply by making your team members more aware of security issues. Asking your checkout person to double-check each item before dropping it in the plastic bag, making sure price tags are correct, seeing that shelves aren't overpacked, or taking care that the correct products are dispatched will go a long way towards reducing stock losses.

Confirm Details before Service or Product Delivery

Having to redo an order or resend it has got to be the fastest way to make you broke.

Stupid errors like getting the wrong delivery address or the wrong town could prove very costly. Not only could orders get lost and cost you money, but they could also be delivered to the wrong address and accepted there. In this case, you would have to eat the loss and resend the order. Your customers would be most unhappy, especially if the orders were urgently needed. They might decide to change to a competitor.

Institute a system that double-checks delivery address details. It's a simple fix for a potentially expensive problem.

Use a *Just-in-Time* Stock Delivery System

This system makes sure that you not only get the stock, but that you get it just before it's needed.

Efficiency in this area can save you a fortune. Inefficiency here can cost you your business. It's all about careful monitoring and forecasting. It's the ideal scenario for a computer-based system. So use one.

Talk to your salespeople; they know their market. They also know what orders have just been placed, what are likely to be coming in shortly, and when times of high or low demand can be expected. Tap into this intelligence and use it to drive your stock levels.

Testing and Measuring

I'm going to say this once again: Test and measure everything. Make it part of your daily business routine. And I know most business people hate doing it. This is because it means there is a chance, however remote, that what they have been doing isn't working. In other words, it is possible that they'll discover that they've been spending money without seeing any returns.

That makes this business of testing and measuring pretty unattractive to most people.

But consider this: You've probably been testing and measuring all your business life. Remember the newspaper advertising you tried that didn't work, and the radio spots that did OK?

That's all testing is.

The next step is to do it properly. Here's how in basic terms:

Step 1

Monitor what you're currently doing. Of course, I'm talking about monitoring that area of your business that you want to test and measure. Make sense? For instance, if you wanted to test and measure the efficiency of your delivery system, you'd be monitoring what goes on in your dispatch department. You could do this by asking questions and taking notes, having a questionnaire completed by those that work there, or having a series of checklists completed over a set period of time.

Step 2

Prune, modify, and increase what is currently being done, depending on the results you get. Note the results this has on what you're testing and measuring.

Step 3

Test and measure for another two weeks.

Step 4

Check how the results pan out. Has there been an improvement?

Step 5

Consolidate. Let things stand as they are for a month or two.

Step 6

Branch out and implement another strategy or try something new to improve results. You are aiming for continual improvement.

So, what general strategies can you implement as far as systems are concerned? Here are some suggestions.

Complete and Keep to Monthly and Yearly Budgets

Cashflow is what usually kills business. Or, to be more precise, the lack of cashflow. Know where yours is going as regularly as possible.

The key to ensuring that your business maximizes its cashflow is to complete, and stick to, regular budgets. Budgeting makes sense. It's also good business practice, because it allows you to keep your finger on the pulse of your business. If you regularly monitor your cashflow, you will have early warning of impending problems. If cashflow is down according to budget, you need to take immediate action; otherwise your business will run into serious trouble. If cashflow is up, you can divert surplus funds into areas where it can better work for you.

Remember, if you're not concentrating on creating cashflow, then you're wasting your time in business.

Measure Conversion Rates for Each Salesperson

If you do this, you'll know where you've got to improve and exactly how you're performing.

The conversion rate is the difference between those customers who could have bought from you and those that actually did. If 10 people come into your shop and only two buy, the conversion rate is 2 out of 10, or 20 percent. Knowing what the conversion rate is for each salesperson allows you to not only devise plans to increase it; it also allows you to work out how the business is performing and what its potential is. If you're getting by with a 30 percent conversion rate, imagine how your business would run at 70 percent.

You can monitor this in a nonthreatening way by turning it into a sales competition with prizes for those who reach a certain target. Display a large conversion rate chart to record how each salesperson is progressing. Make it the focus of your sales department.

Complete a Purchasing System for All Internal Purchases

Don't let people spend money until they've got an authorized purchase order. Create a simple system for this.

If team members are allowed to go out and make purchases whenever they want to, you will have no control. Not only will you be losing the opportunity to negotiate better prices with suppliers based on volume, you will also be losing control of your cashflow. People might be tempted to buy more expensive items, as they may not be aware that cheaper ones could do the job just as well. Duplication is sure to occur, resulting in higher expenses and a negative impact on your bottom line.

Make sure one person controls the purchase orders. It could be your financial officer, administration manager, or office manager. Centralize this function and it will run more smoothly.

Always Complete a Marketing Campaign Profit Analysis

The aim here is to know where you're making money and where you're losing it.

If you spend money on marketing, do you know whether or not it's working? Do you have any idea how much every new customer costs you? Do you know how much you are losing making that first sale to a new customer? And do you know when that customer becomes profitable to you?

One simple way to find answers to these fundamental business questions is to analyze your marketing campaigns. You need to compare the total cost of each campaign with the number of new customers it brings in. Develop a simple questionnaire or get each salesperson to ask some questions and keep notes. Then record each purchase. This will allow you to analyze whether you're making a profit or losing money.

Once you know this, it's then just a matter of fine-tuning your campaigns, dropping them, or keeping them running.

Complete a Petty Cash System

You don't have to write a check for everything just because you want to keep a record of what you spend, but be sure to keep receipts.

It's all about being in control of your cashflow. Develop a simple system that allows you to issue petty cash when it's needed. You can appoint someone to be responsible for this function. Issue them with a receipt book and decide on a procedure. Then let everyone know what the procedure is and who controls the petty cash.

Keep a Record of Your Profit Margins

Know what your big margin products and services are and focus on them. It's not just about turnover; it's also about profit.

Remember, *profit is king.* You need to know which products or services bring in the most profit, because it usually takes just as much effort to sell highly profitable items as it does to sell something with low profit margins. Concentrate on what's good for the business first, then the less profitable items will be the icing on the cake.

Continuously Measure the Number and Origin of All Leads

It's a basic business principle that the more you know the easier it is to make decisions about what's working and what's not.

Few businesses know how many leads they get each week. Even fewer know where those leads came from. Develop a database and keep in regular contact with leads. Work on converting these leads to customers. If you get the same number of leads whether you run a marketing campaign or not, you need to rethink your campaign. But you'll never know if you're not continuously measuring the number and origin of the leads you get.

Constantly Monitor Credit Control and the Age of Your Accounts

You're not a bank so don't go loaning people money. Rather than allowing them time to pay, give them an incentive for early payment.

If you monitor the age of your accounts, you will soon see which ones pay on time and which are in the habit of getting way overdue. Remember, the name of the game is cashflow. If the cash owed to you isn't coming in regularly when due, it'll be to the detriment of your business. It will be costing you money.

Work on getting money owed to you in when it's due, even if this means offering incentives. Try offering a small percentage discount for prompt payment. The cost of offering a discount is definitely outweighed by the consequences of having large amounts of money outstanding.

Measure Your Average Dollar Sale for Every Team Member

One of the things you need to know is who's making the money and who needs training.

Knowing what the average dollar sale is for your business as a whole will allow you to quickly and easily keep your finger on your estimated profit. It will give you an insight into what needs to be focused on to increase the overall profitability of your business.

You see, it you wanted to increase the profitability of your business, all you then need to do is to increase the average dollar sale for all team members. But unless you know what their average dollar sale is to start with, how will you know what they need to aim for and whether they've made improvements or not? You need to establish a starting point.

This is also an excellent indicator as to who could benefit from training or retraining. It's also a great motivational device, because a poorly performing sales force would be able to track changes in their performance before and after training. It couldn't be easier.

Record the Number of Transactions for Each Customer

If your customers are coming back, then this is a great thing to know and measure.

A simple system will tell you how many times customers buy from you, when they buy, what they buy, and how much they spend. This data will prove invaluable for future marketing campaigns. It will also be invaluable to you when you implement campaigns aimed at building customer loyalty.

Remember, hanging onto existing customers is far cheaper than finding new ones. But unless you have the data, how will you know whether they are new or existing customers? You won't.

Complete a Monthly Balance Sheet

Know your worth and whether the picture gets better or worse each and every month.

A monthly balance sheet is a snapshot of the health of your business. It'll tell you whether the things you are doing are working or not. It'll tell you whether you need to be thinking about doing things differently. And, if you are building up your company, the monthly balance sheet is an excellent indicator of the rate at which your company is growing.

So many business people think the balance sheet is something only the accountant or bookkeeper should be concerned with. What rubbish. Learn how to read it, learn what its function is, and understand the signals it gives. You see, the balance sheet is in reality a multifunctional business tool because apart from its obvious function, it's also an early warning tool that is able to forecast looming trouble. Use it wisely and you'll save yourself a whole lot of aggravation and trouble.

Measure Key Performance Indicators in All Areas of the Company

You cannot manage what you do not measure. Make sure everyone measures their Key Performance Indicators.

Set individual targets and link them to bonuses. That will give individual team members something positive to strive for. It also adds an element of competition into their daily routines.

By doing this, you will also be ensuring that people aim for, and achieve, their own individual goals. This will not only have positive effects on the running of your business, it will have positive effects on your team members as well.

Complete a Weekly Bank Reconciliation

You need to know whether you're on track with your accounting and that your bank's doing a good job.

Reconciling your bank account, on a weekly basis, allows you to quickly pick up any errors or misallocations that could be costing you money. It will help pinpoint internal record-keeping mistakes due to wrongly allocating codes or entering the wrong pricing. You can then tighten up on the appropriate system.

Weekly reconciliations also allow you to monitor your cashflow.

Daily or Weekly Update Your Cashflow Statements

Poor cashflow is what usually kills business after business. To help ensure that you don't become another statistic, you need to know where your cash is going as regularly as possible. You need to have your finger on its pulse. Is more coming in than going out, or is it the other way around?

If you have good systems in place, you should know what your cashflow is doing. By updating your cashflow statements on a daily basis, not only will you have the very best information available at you fingertips; it'll also save you time and effort. It's much easier entering a few transactions on a daily basis rather than a large amount weekly or monthly. There'll be fewer errors, too.

The sooner you get warning of a looming cashflow crisis, the sooner you can make plans to avoid or counteract it. You'll be more in control of your business and able to direct its growth, rather than having to spend time sorting out crisis after crisis. You'll be acting in a proactive rather than reactive manner.

Have a Daily Banking System

Get your money into the bank with 100 percent accuracy, as soon as possible.

That way, not only will it be safe, it can also start working for you. Furthermore, banking on a daily basis involves less accounting in the long run and ensures that there is less chance of mistakes being made.

Remember cash in the bank equals cashflow. Your bank manager will love you if you get in the habit of doing your banking on a daily basis.

Complete Regular Stock Control Checkups

As an accountant, you've got to make sure the numbers are always accurate. .

It's far easier to measure small amounts on a regular basis than a large amount once in a while. Errors due to fatigue, confusion, and boredom can easily creep in if you handle one massive stock control check each year. More frequent checkups also act as early warning signs and can point to existing or upcoming problems.

Complete All Regular Government Returns

Nothing will hit harder than a government return not filed on time. Make sure that you or your accountant follows this through.

If you are conducting regular stock control checkups, completing monthly balance sheets, reconciling regularly with your bank, and keeping on top of your cashflow statements, you should have no trouble completing regular government returns on time. Build this into your system, and include it in your bookkeeper's (or other responsible person's) Key Performance Indicators. There should be no excuse for not meeting the deadline.

Keep an Asset Register That Includes Depreciation

You need to know what you own, serial numbers and all. Most importantly, you need to know how much each item you own is worth.

This is a simple, yet very effective, step to take to know the real value of your business. Do it early on: It'll save you much heartache and effort when it comes to meeting your tax obligations at the end of the financial year. After all, you must claim all the tax breaks you can get—they are there for the taking. It also proves beneficial later should you decide to sell your business.

Work with an External Accountant for Tax Planning

Good accountants will never cost you money; they will save it for you. But make sure you're working with good accountants.

Make their job easier by providing them with as much up-to-date information as you can. This is where having good business systems will pay dividends.

Have a System for Payroll and Superannuation

It shouldn't take you long at all to process your payroll and make superannuation payments if you're following a simple and easy-to-use system. But if you find this all a little overwhelming, then you should consider outsourcing this function.

You need to bear in mind that, from an employee's point of view, this is what it's all about. They are, after all, usually only working because they need the money. Nothing will upset them as much as not depositing their salaries or wages into their bank accounts on time. A late payment can cause untold inconvenience, not to mention cost and embarrassment, as automatic deductions could default and penalties be incurred.

Remember, employees trade time for money. They've put in the time; now you need to ensure that your side of the deal is honored.

Systems and Technology

These days with the ever-changing and rapidly quickening pace of technological developments, you really do need to keep on top of things in this respect if you hope to stay in control of this aspect of your business. But don't let it frighten you. It's not that difficult to do. All you need to ensure is that you have good systems in place to begin with, then it will take care of itself.

So take a close look at what you can do to simplify matters. This area is all about systems and technology, an area ideally suited to being systemized.

So where do you start? Here are some quick and easy suggestions.

Schedule and Complete Regular Maintenance on All Equipment

Rather than waiting until your machinery crashes, get it serviced in times of low need.

It'll also cost you less in the long run. Regular routine maintenance will not only keep your machinery running in tip-top condition for longer periods of time, it'll also save you money by not having to endure long periods of costly nonproductive downtime.

Bear in mind too that if you neglect to look after your equipment as specified by the manufacturer, you could also affect your manufacturer's warranties and insurance policies.

So start by checking what the maintenance requirements are for all machinery and other pieces of equipment you have. These include motor vehicles, manufacturing machinery, office equipment such as copy machines, printing machines, and generators. There could be others.

Use Computer Invoicing and Credit Monitoring

Save yourself time and money, and be sure that everything is consistent.

There are many excellent computer systems available that run everything from invoicing to bank account balances. They are simple to use and consistent. They will also monitor overdue payments and issue statements for you. Use them; they'll save you time and money.

Document and Picture All Tasks in an Operations Manual

This has already been covered at length under "People and Education," but I'll go over it again here as it does overlap into this category.

You need to document what needs to be done, when it needs to be done, who should do it, what the standards are, and how to measure the results.

This is important, as it not only sets out how each task is to be done, it states what the standards are, what happens when things go wrong, and how team members can monitor and measure their progress. Think of the operations manual as the definitive guide on how things are done in your business. It is a step-by-step guide to getting the job done, with illustrations and photographs where applicable.

Operations manuals also reassure your employees that they are doing things correctly and *in accordance with the book.* It lets them know what the standards are and what's expected of them. It helps avoid internal conflict by acting as the standard by which things are done.

Introduce all new employees to the operations manual during their initial induction training.

Run a Computerized Stock Control System

Don't leave it to chance. You can do with one computer what five or six people used to do.

Stock control is one area of your business that lends itself to computerization. Tie in everything from ordering stock, pricing, and stock replenishment, to inventory control into the same system. Make sure you operate on the just-in-time stock purchasing principle. It couldn't be easier. And it's more accurate.

Complete Systems Training and an Induction Program

Training people how to use a good system takes about a tenth of the time it takes to teach people how to do the job.

Remember, systems run the business and people run the systems. So invest some time and money into training and your business will flourish. Start training your people right from the beginning by including systems training in the induction program. That way you can establish a systems culture in your business. If your team members become convinced about the benefits of a systems approach, they will begin to monitor the systems they are involved with in an intimate way. They will be able to make suggestions about how to change, fine-tune, or improve the system as the working environment changes. This way, things couldn't be better and your business will go from strength to strength.

You'll really have a situation where the systems run your business, while your people run the systems.

Use the Latest Computer Programs

One of the drawbacks of using computer software in the workplace is that you really have to keep up with technological developments. There are good reasons for this. Software companies really do keep updating their packages for your good (as well as theirs, of course). Newer, more efficient tools are constantly being added to enhance the benefits for you, the user.

But that's not the only compelling reason to keep up-to-date with the latest software packages as they hit the market. You need to maintain your businesses capacity to deal with, or work with, electronic work flowing in and out of your business. You need to ensure that your work is compatible with that of other businesses.

Sure, your primary objective as far as computing is concerned may just be to produce simple, unsophisticated Word documents, but unless you keep pace with the introduction of new word-processing packages, the time will come when your system and its programs are no longer supported by the major software suppliers. This means businesses that use the latest packages will not be able to read yours, should you have to e-mail them. Your e-mail facility will also be severely affected as you wouldn't have the latest packages for downloads.

Chances are that the members of your team will be keeping pace with developments and will begin to feel that they are working for a conservative, backward-thinking company, especially if their private computer setup at home is more up-to-date than the one they use at work.

So, ensure that you keep your computer systems up-to-date. This way it's easy for everyone to use them and there's great training available. Another advantage is that new people joining your business will probably know the programs as well. You see, chances are they'll be more familiar with the latest programs than with older, outdated ones.

It's all about consistency. There's nothing worse than not being able to use certain software packages or not being able to open a simple document just because you're running outdated software. Being up-to-date also sends out a positive message about your company.

Every time you install a new software package, it's a good opportunity to hold a training session. This also serves as a good opportunity for team building.

Complete a Phone/Fax Systems Upgrade

Technology saves you so much time when you use it well. And in business, time is money.

Having the latest technology may also be more cost-effective. Often, one new piece of equipment takes the place of three older pieces. Gone are the days when you needed to have separate telephone, fax machine, printer, and photocopier. You can now get one machine that does all this. It's cheaper and it saves space too. These modern machines work better and you'll experience less down time. Be sure to consider the fact that some phone systems will transfer to mobile phones as well.

Go Through and Regularly Update Quality Control/Assurance

Once you have systems in place, the very least you'll have is everything you need to run your business on paper. Now it's just a matter of following through.

Change is the only constant. Your business and political environment, the economy, and even fashions and fads change over time. All these uncontrollable factors are sure to have an effect on the way you do business. They can even challenge the very existence of your business, unless you are prepared to adapt.

Systems and procedures need to be reviewed and amended to suit changing conditions and requirements. Be sure to reflect these changes in your quality control or assurance manuals or procedures. It's simple, but it's easily overlooked.

Run a Computer Backup System

This can save a mountain of time should the worst happen to your computers.

Computers can and do crash, and they usually do so at the most inconvenient times. Losing all your data isn't just infuriating, it can also cost you everything. Having a backup system can be extremely simple. It can be as easy as getting your people to transfer their files or data onto disc at the end of each day.

There are many sophisticated systems available, ranging from downloads onto tape to the automatic electronic transfer of information to a safe remote site each evening. Make enquiries if you don't already have a backup system in place. You'll be pleasantly surprised at how cost-effective it really is. And if you do have a backup system, then think about having an outside consultant run a computer security audit for you. You may find that what you're doing isn't adequate or that there may be a far better and cheaper system you should be using. Either way, you must back up your information.

Run Both Internal and External E-Mail

As long as people don't go crazy, it'll save you mountains of time and energy.

Sending information internally via e-mail isn't only efficient and fast; it is also cheap. In fact, it's far cheaper than manually distributing office memorandums or letters. Another advantage of making use of electronic distribution channels is that the sender knows that it's been delivered. There's also an electronic record kept of it, so it saves storage space as well. You can set up an *all staff* e-mail group to make distribution simple. You can also establish department groups, groups that run along seniority lines, or you can send e-mails individually to members of your team.

Document and Chart All Work Flow Processes

Do you know the path *work* takes through your business? You see, to be really successful, you've got to know what follows what, and where everything should go next. I know this is putting it simply, but work does have a flow path in every business. Think of it like the flow of an electric current through an electric circuit. Electronic technicians refer to a schematic diagram so they can diagnose faults in items of electronic equipment like television sets, home entertainment systems, and radios.

The same principle applies to business. Drawing up a flowchart of your various work processes will help you to clearly understand the mechanics of your business. It will assist in pinpointing bottlenecks and things that could be done better and more easily. It will also assist new team members in finding their feet quicker and help everyone be more productive.

Of course, having this flowchart also makes it easy to write how-to operational manuals.

Document All Sales and Marketing Systems

If you have a sales and marketing campaign that worked, then it's a system you want to work with for the rest of the time. And why wouldn't you?

It's no good running a sales and marketing system that doesn't work. It also doesn't make sense running a system that you don't know works. So if you have a system that works, document everything you do in this regard so it can be repeated again and again. This will lead to consistency and save you time and money as it brings in the results.

Document Information Flow Processes

As long as it's on paper, it's probably got to go somewhere and have someone do something with it. Write down where each piece of paper goes, and then anyone can handle it.

There's no point having cupboards full of reports and memos if nobody ever makes use of them. Cluttered shelves and drawers are a waste of time and money.

You need to realize that information is the lifeblood of business. Understanding how it flows in your business is crucial to running a good business. Information overload, lack of crucial information, misunderstandings, and being unable to interpret information are problems that can have a very significant effect on your business and something you need to sort out quickly and satisfactorily.

By documenting its flow path, you'll save everyone time and heartache. You'll be more organized, and so will your people and your business.

Use a Purpose-Designed Computer Database Program

Manage your customers, their buying patterns, and your business through your computer.

It always astounds me how little most business owners know about their customers. Even fewer know anything about their leads. Developing a computer database of your leads is simple, yet it could very well turn out to be one of the most powerful tools you'll have.

Collect as much information as you can about your leads, and then add to it as they become customers. Develop it as time goes by. Get your salespeople to routinely ask questions that will add to your database; "Where did you hear about us?" "Do you mind if I write down your contact details?" and "What is your number-one concern with the product you're currently using?" The list of questions is endless and should be tailored to meet your requirements. And by the way, most people don't mind leaving their contact details, if they're to be used ethically. Let them know that it's to put them on your mailing list so they can be among the first to know about new products, sales, or special offers.

It's as simple as that.

Create a database, starting with all your leads, and develop from there. Include names and contact details, as well as information relating to their buying behavior and patterns. This information will become the central core of information for your business. It will be priceless. Use it to easily increase your profit.

Network All Computers for Ease of Access

File sharing, printer sharing, and running a networked system means you have to change it only once if you need to implement upgrades, additions, or corrections.

Networks make the sharing of information simple and efficient. It also saves money, as there's no longer a need to print out documents to pass around. You can save on the number of peripheral printers and fax machines you need to run. Instead of running many medium-quality printers, you can run one good-quality laser printer that is connected to all your computers through the network. And when it comes to updates, you need to do this only once, as everyone on the network will automatically have access to it.

Use Rosters and Schedules for Repetitive Tasks

Focus on the routine getting done without anyone really noticing, and then you're able to really focus on the customer.

Nobody likes doing repetitive tasks, but unfortunately, they still need to be done. So spread them around and let everyone do a little. That way everyone shares a lighter load.

What kinds of tasks do I have in mind? Things like washing up in the lunch room. This task has to be done; yet it doesn't directly affect the company's bottom line. It sure makes life a lot easier, and it doesn't automatically belong to any specific functional area. If everyone takes a turn at doing it, each person might only get the washing up duties once a month, but that's better than some person having to do it three times a day, every day.

By instituting a fair system to take care of these routine, mundane tasks, you'll also be emphasizing the importance of teamwork.

Complete a Policies and Procedures Manual

If everything's written down, then duplication is a simple step and you're reliant on the system, not the people.

The key to developing a successful business is to develop a set of systems that runs the business. Systems ensure that things run smoothly, every time. The systems are recorded in a set of manuals, known as the policy and procedure manuals. They are the main reference books for the business.

Complete a Machinery Automation and Upgrade

There's one thing you have to admit about machinery: If it does the job a whole lot better and faster, then it's probably cheaper and more reliable in the long run.

But remember, machinery needs to be maintained and upgraded from time to time. Build this into your system and review it regularly. Technological advances provide benefits that include the automation of various tasks as well as cost savings and better levels of precision. Are you missing out?

Document All Accounting Systems

It's far better to have a system and an unskilled person working for you than no system and a highly skilled person who may leave at any minute.

Accounting systems are easy to use, once they have been set up. What's more, everyone can also use them; much of the data input can, in any case, come directly from other interacting systems such as sales and marketing, inventory, purchasing, and operations. If your accounting system is well designed and documented, anyone should be able to use it.

Upgrade Office Equipment Regularly

If it's going to assist in productivity, then you're probably saving and not spending by upgrading.

Having the latest in office equipment not only assists your business by being more efficient; it makes your people feel good as well. Morale is better and productivity will certainly be higher. It's also good for your image.

Prioritize Extraordinary Tasks

Extraordinary tasks can be time-consuming and costly to deal with. Can your system cope with them?

Prioritize extraordinary tasks as they occur. Get them sorted out as soon as possible and remember to upgrade your systems and manuals accordingly, by taking them into account. That way, the next time they occur they won't be extraordinary tasks any more.

Use these as team-building exercises if possible. They can be carried out during slack periods or after hours, depending on their nature. If extraordinary tasks happen regularly, revisit your systems and fine-tune where necessary, because there are too many gaps in your system.

Resystem as Your Company Grows

As your company grows, your systems may be tested to the limit of their original design, rendering them outdated, inefficient, or unable to cope. They may be no longer relevant and workable.

Review and audit your systems as your business grows. It's far easier amending or adapting a system as you grow, rather than starting from scratch and developing a completely new one to cater to a very different set of circumstances.

Security Systems

How secure is your business? Can it survive a major robbery or even a computer crash?

Theft, industrial espionage, and shrinkage are becoming major problems for business owners the world over. What would you do if you were the target of an organized gang? What would you do if your computer network were infected with a debilitating computer virus? Are these possibilities catered to by your security system? Conduct regular audits and consult with external professionals to ensure that you are not at risk. Or at least that your risk is minimized. Discuss options with your insurance company, fire department, and police service (if applicable). Doing so may even qualify you for an insurance discount.

```
┌──────────────┐
│    Part 4    │
└──────────────┘
```

■ The Nine Steps to Systemizing Your Business

What I have discussed until now is how you'd go about developing systems for an existing business. But what if you are just about to start building or establishing a new business? Would it be any different?

In many cases it's probably a whole lot easier to systemize a brand new business, because you won't have to *undo* existing or entrenched methods or ways of doing things. But of course, much of what we've already covered will still be most relevant. So if you are just starting out in business or if you are establishing a new business, then congratulations. You couldn't be reading this book at a better time.

So, your aim is to build a business. Let's stop here for a moment and consider just what it is you're aiming to do. What is a business? Perhaps I should be more specific. What is my definition of a business?

A *business* is a commercial, profitable enterprise that works without you. Now, consider this: What is the difference between a business and a promotion? Many business people just have a promotion and go through life thinking it's a business. Let me explain. In a promotion, you have one product, one service, and once you've sold it to someone, that's it. You've got to go out and find yourself another customer. That's an ongoing marketing promotion, not a business. On the other hand, a business is where you buy customers and then sell something, or many things, to them over and over and over again.

And one other thing: When you build a business, you build it with the end in mind. In other words, you build it according to how you envision it when it is finished. This is very important, because it affects everything you do in your building stage. Your vision, mission and goals will have to take this into account. You see, let me explain by using the vision of my company, *Action International* as an example. My vision is World Abundance Through Business Reeducation.

Notice it's *world* abundance, not *Australian* or *South-east Queensland* abundance. This sets the tone for the whole company and its future. It also dictates how others see us.

At the outset you need to consider this: Why do most business owners work so hard? The simple answer is because their businesses don't work. You see, if their businesses did work, they really wouldn't have to work hard at all. And there's another compelling reason why you need to make sure your business works. It's this: If you have a carpentry business that doesn't work (and by work I mean work without you), if you decided to sell it, the only person you could sell it to would be another carpenter. Now what sort of price do you think you'd be able to achieve? Not very much at all. But what if the business did work? You'd then be able to sell it to people because they wouldn't actually be required to work in the business. It would be set up to work without them. Suddenly your market would be very much bigger, with investors becoming likely prospects. Now you'd be able to charge very much more for the business. Ray Kroc of McDonald's fame once said that you must build your business as if it will be replicated thousands upon thousands of times. This would ensure that it would be able to work without you, simply because you wouldn't be able to work in them all at the same time. You'd have to develop good systems to run the business for you.

And one last tip: When building a business, do it systematically. Work your way through the following nine steps:

Step 1: Vision

This is the long-term goal of your business. And by long term, I mean 100 years. Don't mess around with short-term goals here. We're talking about the grand picture of what your business will be like when it's finished.

Here once again is the vision of *Action International:*

The Vision You'll Support ...

World Abundance Through Business Reeducation ...

When I visit various businesses I often ask the person that greets me at the entrance what the company's vision is. I invariably get a blank stare. "Oh, it must be that thing that hangs on the wall in the boss's office." Understand that this just isn't good enough. Every single person in the business needs to know exactly what the company's vision is. Furthermore, team members all need to identify with it and accept it as their vision too. Whenever I recruit new team members, the very first thing I discuss with them is our vision. I let them know what we are striving for. If they can't identify with that, I tell them they're welcome to leave then and there.

Step 2: Mission Statement

The mission statement states how your business is going to accomplish its vision. It is obviously very much more detailed than the vision statement. It should clearly spell out the following:

- Who you are.

- What business you are in.

- Who your customers are.

- What makes you different from your competition.

This last point is very important. It's something you need to spend time getting clear in your own mind first. You see, the day you differentiate yourself from the rest, you won't have to compete on price any more. That's why a Giorgio Armani shirt costs very much more than one from K-Mart. I mean they might very well be made from the same material and in the same factory, but the Giorgio Armani costs more precisely because of marketing differentiation.

Here's my *Action International* Mission Statement:

The Mission Statement You'll Embody ...

Action International is a team of committed, positive, and successful people who are always striving to be balanced, integrated, and honest. We will work within our "14 Points of Culture" to make sure that all who touch or are touched by the *Action International* team will benefit greatly and in some way move closer to becoming the people they want to be or achieve the goals they want to achieve.

We will always work in co-opetition with all those who believe they are in competition with us.

We are in the business of Edutainment. We will educate ourselves, our clients, and all those whom we work with, while we entertain them and create a fun learning environment. We will educate our clients in world-class marketing and business development techniques using audio, video, CDs, other technologies and simple workbooks, workshops, and seminar formats.

Our products and services will be of the highest quality, value for money, and whether sourced from within the company or externally will always add the most value and use the latest and most effective training methodologies available.

ActionCOACH clients, whether they be small, medium, or large in size will have a desire to have us help them in achieving their goals and be able to take on Our Commitment to them by returning Their Commitment to **ActionCOACH.** They will be forward thinking, willing to learn and grow, and be willing to work as team players in the development of an organization of *people*.

Our clients will be selected more on attitude than size, and they will want to deal with us because we understand that people are important, systems should run a company, we offer the most practical, most applicable, and fastest strategies of growth, and most importantly because we mean what we say.

We will give people back their spirit and freedom through business development.

The Uniqueness You'll Help to Position **ActionCOACH** with ...

The World's Most Practical Marketing and Business Development because Being in Business should Give You More life ...

Once again, this is discussed with every applicant during the interview process. It is explained and talked about at length. Applicants are given the opportunity to ask questions and to say if they feel comfortable or uncomfortable with it. If they don't agree with it or feel it doesn't excite them, they are invited to leave and look for a business that better suits their outlook.

Step 3: Culture Statement

This is generally a 14-point statement that includes the following:

- Your four most important values as leader of the company

- Your team's four most important values

- Your customer's four most important values

This is discussed at length with all new team members at the time of their initial interview. Doing so saves us a whole lot of time and helps us find people that will fit in well with the rest of the team. We always find the right people from day one as a result.

This is our Culture Statement:

Action's **14 Points of Culture**

Commitment I give myself and everything I commit to 100 percent until I succeed. I am committed to the Vision, Mission, Culture, and success of *Action International,* its current and future team, and its clients at all times. I always recommend products and services of *Action International* prior to going outside the company.

Ownership I am truly responsible for my actions and outcomes and own everything that takes place in my work and my life. I am accountable for my results and I know that for things to change, first I must change.

Integrity I always speak the truth. What I promise is what I deliver. I only ever make agreements with myself and others that I am willing and intend to keep. I communicate potential broken agreements at the first opportunity and I clear up all broken agreements immediately.

Excellence Good enough isn't. I always deliver products and services of exceptional quality that add value to all involved for the long term. I look for ways to do more with less and stay on a path of constant and never-ending improvement and innovation.

Bradley J. Sugars

Communication I speak positively of my fellow team members, my clients, and *Action International* in both public and private. I speak with good purpose using empowering and positive conversation. I never use or listen to sarcasm or gossip. I acknowledge what is being said as true for the speaker at that moment and I take responsibility for responses to my communication. I greet and say good-bye to people using their names. I always apologize for any upsets first and then look for a solution. I only ever discuss concerns in private with the person involved.

Success I totally focus my thoughts, energy, and attention on the successful outcome of whatever I am doing. I am willing to win and allow others to win: Win/Win. At all times, I display my inner pride, prosperity, competence, and personal confidence. I am a successful person.

Education I learn from my mistakes. I consistently learn, grow, and master so that I can help my fellow team members and clients learn, grow, and master too. I am an educator and allow my clients to make their own intelligent decisions about their future, remembering that it is their future. I impart practical and useable knowledge rather than just theory.

Teamwork I am a team player and team leader. I do whatever it takes to stay together and achieve team goals. I focus on cooperation and always come to a resolution, not a compromise. I am flexible in my work and able to change if what I'm doing is not working. I ask for help when I need it and I am compassionate to others who ask me.

Balance I have a balanced approach to life, remembering that my spiritual, social, physical, and family aspects are just as important as my financial and intellectual. I complete my work and my most important tasks first, so I can have quality time to myself, with my family, and also to renew.

Fun I view my life as a journey to be enjoyed and appreciated and

I create an atmosphere of fun and happiness so all around me enjoy it as well.

Systems
I always look to the system for a solution. If a challenge arises I use a system correction before I look for a people correction. I use a system solution in my innovation rather than a people solution. I follow the system exactly until a new system is introduced. I suggest system improvements at my first opportunity.

Consistency
I am consistent in my actions so my clients and teammates can feel comfortable in dealing with me at all times. I am disciplined in my work so my results, growth, and success are consistent.

Gratitude
I am a truly grateful person. I say thank-you and show appreciation often and in many ways, so that all around me know how much I appreciate everything and everyone I have in my life. I celebrate my wins and the wins of my clients and team. I consistently catch myself and other people doing things right.

Abundance
I am an abundant person. I deserve my abundance and I am easily able to both give and receive it. I allow abundance in all areas of my life by respecting my own self-worth and that of all others. I am rewarded to the level that I create abundance for others, and I accept that abundance only shows up in my life to the level at which I show up.

Step 4: Goals

It's your goals that help you achieve your vision. And because of the long-term nature of your vision, your goals should have varying time frames. When setting your goals, you need to bear the following in mind:

- You must set *SMART* goals. They need to be *Specific*, *Measurable*, *Achievable*, *Results*-oriented, and have a *Time* frame.

- You must set a goal that tells you when you're going to finish the business—when it will work without you.

- Your goals give you and the business direction and focus; they create movement and momentum and the person (or business) you become because of your goals. This last point is important because if you had a goal to become a world player, you'd become a very different person than if your goal was to become a major player in your town.

Step 5: Organizational Chart

You need to decide what positions there will be in your business when it's finished. No, not when you start it, but when it's finished. You need to plan this all up front. Sure you can grow into it over time, but if you don't envision the finished company now, you run the risk of painting yourself into a corner and closing certain avenues or options before you get there.

Step 6: Positional Contracts

It's very important to tell your people what they're supposed to be doing. Spell it out in clear, unambiguous terms. There's nothing more daunting for new team members than arriving on their first day and being unsure about what they are expected to do. They will be confused enough without this added burden.

Having positional contracts will also save you the agony of sorting out involved and emotionally charged disputes that arise through misunderstandings relating to what a person should or shouldn't be doing. This is particularly so when things go wrong in the workplace and fingers start being pointed.

Step 7: KPIs

You should have Key Performance Indicators for every position. Generally speaking, there should be no less than 5 and no more than 10 for each position. You see, if team members have 30 KPIs and they don't perform on one, what's one out of 30? It becomes meaningless.

Set bonuses based on the attainment of the KPIs. Let me give you an example: I owned a photocopy business once in which one of the KPIs for all team members was to wear their uniform perfectly every day. If they all did, the entire team would receive a $10 bonus for the week. Well, on the first day someone didn't wear the name tag so the entire team missed out on that week's bonus. The team very quickly produced two name tags for each person; one to take home and one for the office, in case someone arrived at work without a name tag. From that moment on they were always dressed and always earned their bonuses.

Step 8: How-to Manuals

This has already been discussed at length, so I won't go through it in detail again. However, you need to remember that how-to manuals don't have to be written down. They can be on video or audiotape or anything else that serves the purpose.

A friend of mine runs a restaurant and he used photos to show how he wanted the kitchens to look at all times. It worked very well for him. The thing to remember here is that if it becomes easier not to use the system, you have a bad system. You need to ensure that it is always easier to use the system than to ignore it. Keep this in mind when designing yours.

Step 9: Milestones

Consider these the major landmarks that you'll pass along the way while building your business; they are the main stages the business will reach on its journey from infancy to maturity and adulthood.

Your milestones could be the opening of your first office, the opening of your first branch, or the opening of your first international head office. It could also be moving out of rented premises into your first business-owned building, or hiring your first managing director.

Of course, every business will have many milestones that need to be incorporated. Some will be more momentous than others, but they'll all be important in the life of the business. You could set financial milestones such as passing the $1 million mark in profit or becoming a million dollar business. The next financial milestone might be becoming a deca-million dollar business, then a billion dollar business. You could include milestones that focus on the number of people who work for the business, the number of retail outlets it has, or the date when it becomes a franchise operation. It all depends on the nature and vision of your business, but the opportunities really are limitless. Think carefully and be as specific as you can.

These then are the nine steps you need to take to systemize a new business. Work through them systematically and thoroughly. They will pay dividends and save you loads of time in the long run. I have found that for every system I wrote, I saved myself five minutes of work. I didn't have to write too many systems to save myself the whole week.

Some Real Examples

It's time now for some more real examples. You see, I can talk all I want about how to do it, what to do, and why, but unless I illustrate this by means of real examples, the real message of just how dramatic the introduction of systems to a business is may be lost.

So let me give you two great examples at this point. One concerns one of my own businesses, and the other is a case study of an *Action* Coach. Both will give you a good insider's look at the impact systems have on a business.

My Photocopy Shop Business

I first fell in love with systems when I bought my photocopy business. We had a string of photocopy shops, and it wasn't long before I noticed that our most senior people weren't in the shops. They were in the office doing paperwork and answering the phones. This I thought counterproductive, so I set out to find out what all the phone calls were about. I discovered that there were basically only 22 reasons why people phoned in, so I sat down and wrote 23 scripts.

Yes, I wrote 23: Twenty-two to cover the reasons they phoned and one to cover any other reason. The last one was simple. It said, "If the reason they phone isn't covered by the 22 scripts, then transfer the caller to a senior person who will be able to answer the query."

I then hired a 16-year-old girl to answer the phone and spent half an hour running her through the scripts. This freed up the senior people to concentrate on their paperwork and not have to worry about the phones.

I then set about delving into what type of paperwork they were doing and discovered that there were only 30 different types. I then bought 30 in-trays from the local stationery shop and typed up a set of instructions to cover each. I then color-coded the trays.

I then wrote a set of manuals, one for each day of the week. This is how simple it was and it bought me back my time. Within four months, I was working for only one hour a day. Isn't that a powerful lesson?

This exercise taught me the following on how to write the how-to manuals:

- List every task done in the business.

- Divide them up into routine and one-time tasks. Systemize the routine first.

- Divide the tasks into daily, weekly, and monthly tasks. Start with the daily because these are the things people do most often.

Now it's time to take a look at the case of a café in New Zealand. It's a terrific story and will show you just what can be done, particularly with the aid of a Business Coach to help you along. This is a real story, as told by the business owner and the Coach. There are no punches pulled and they tell it all.

Café Owners Make Spare Time for Themselves— and More Money

Name:	Café Istanbul
Address:	156 Cuba Street, Wellington, New Zealand
Owners:	Wendy East and Cengiz Altinkaya
Type of Business:	Restaurant
Business Sector:	Food & Beverage/Service
Started:	1991
Coach:	Steve McDonald

The Challenge

The restaurant business has its own unique set of challenges like unsocial working hours, long working days (and nights), and a high turnover of staff. Behind the scenes in the kitchen, there are challenges too concerning stocking levels, choice of menus, preparation time, and the minimization of wastage. The usual result is that restaurant owners don't lead a normal life, resulting all too often in their eventually selling up or burning out.

Fortunately for the owners of Café Istanbul, they decided to take action to ensure that this didn't happen to them. And it so easily could have. You see, their business was stable, but unspectacular. Sales were declining, and there were continual challenges recruiting and retaining a competent team. They were getting good numbers of diners in on Thursdays, Fridays, and Saturdays, but for the remainder of the week, they were operating marginally at best, or at a slight loss.

The owners were working seven nights a week, covering every role in the business. They hadn't had a real break in nine years. And things didn't look like they were changing. If they didn't start doing something differently, they'd be trapped forever, until they either burned out, or walked out.

Wendy's Story

Our business is Café Istanbul. It's a Turkish restaurant in Wellington City. It's a family-owned business that we've run for 11 years now. I look after the front of the house, manage the staff, and see to sales.

Over the last six months to a year, we've noticed a big growth in the upper end of Cuba St., where we are situated. There's a lot more people—a lot more foot traffic, and many bars and cafes are being developed on the street. There are also a lot of inner-city apartments in our area now.

While many of our customers are students, we also cater to those between the ages of 25 and 45; we have quite a few fortieth birthday parties here. We also get twenty-first and even sixtieth and seventieth birthday parties, so our customer base is quite vast.

Our Café is very well known. Everyone in the area knows who we are and where we are. Those who haven't been to us before will always call up to find out. We have a lot of regular customers.

We obviously want to pitch to the people with the most money, so we're thinking of aiming at city dwellers, the apartment people, in the next marketing campaign. These tend to be aged 25 to 35 or 40, have a good disposable income, and probably no children or dependents. They have that extra money to spend on going out.

We're definitely considering opening up for lunch. We have done that once before, but there just wasn't enough foot traffic. But we've noticed in recent times that on a Thursday, Friday, Saturday, and even Sunday there are a lot of people about, and they're all looking for somewhere to have lunch.

We faced several challenges before we met Steve, particularly regarding staffing in the kitchen (we used to import chefs from Turkey), team building with our front-of-house team, and getting the right people. Other challenges included putting systems in place that, perhaps, we hadn't thought of before.

Finding the right staff had always been a big problem. We'd advertise and basically end up just having to take the first available person rather than the right person. Steve has given me some really good information and guidelines on how to choose the right person, rather than be hasty and choose the wrong person, because when running a restaurant, you need people—people on the floor and not just people who are available to work.

In the past, we were basically happy with what we made from the business. Even though we could probably have made a lot more, we didn't try. And with putting different systems in place, like managing our booking times and getting more *butts on seats,* we've been able to increase the number of people we serve, and of course, the number of dollars we take. So there's definitely been a really good increase since we've started working with Steve.

The Moment of Truth

We did think about coaching late last year, but it wasn't until we received a letter from Steve, out of the blue, that we actually thought about it more seriously, and Cengiz and I decided to go ahead with it. It just came at the right time, and he also made a lot of good points in the letter, which caught Cengiz's eye—you know, made him think, "Maybe this guy can help us."

Steve helped us troubleshoot areas and come up with solutions we perhaps wouldn't have thought of. We've got a really good booking management system now, and we've diverted the phone so we take all of the bookings, which we can now manage better. Before, it was left up to the kitchen staff, many of whom could hardly speak English. It was a case of when the restaurant was full, it was full. We also introduced a system to use nightly to allocate tables and direct people to them. We now know who's going where and how long they need at their table. So it's little things like this that have been put together to make the whole running of the restaurant a lot smoother.

There were certainly challenges that we had to overcome along the way. Though most things went together quite well, I know Cengiz had systems to put in place in the kitchen, and he really had to push his team members to do them, because it was something different and they perhaps weren't used to it. In terms of the front-of-house team members, definitely trying to get them to learn how to sell and how to upsell was a challenge, as some of our team members weren't confident in this area.

What have we achieved so far? I'd say there's probably been a 15–20 percent increase in the number of customers we get.

We've also found someone to look after the restaurant on different nights when we're not there. So we've been able to take more time off. Previously we were working six out of seven nights, and as we took alternate nights off, Cengiz and I would hardly ever see each other! So coaching has made it a lot easier. Back then we weren't taking any time off, maybe one night each, but now I've got two or three and Cengiz has four nights off. So we're a lot better off. In the past I would never have been able to sit here, work on systems, and put different things together, whereas before, when I really had to, I didn't have the time to spare.

We are currently training a new team member to become involved in managing the business, so our next challenge is to put systems in place so that he can do it. That's one of the things I have put together: A procedures manual and a team training manual. Our aim is to go overseas next year, so we need to have everything in place so we can actually take the time off.

The Coach's Story

My suggestions included the following:

- Increase prices.

- Train the team to up-sell off the menu.

- Train the team to serve the customer consistently and well.

- Fire the staff that didn't perform and set up a team of great performers.

- Stop recruitment ads that didn't work and advertise for the people they wanted, not the skills they needed.

Our plan of action also included systemizing the kitchen ordering, as well as the day-to-day routines. It was important to make it possible for anyone to open up, shut down, stock the bar, and order kitchen supplies, etc. We also needed to create cleaning, ordering, and maintenance systems, and this work needed to be delegated to team members.

Next we needed to select and groom a manager who could operate the restaurant without the owners needing to be present. Systems were set up to enable this to happen, checklists were then created, as well as a requirements manual and rosters, to ensure that routine tasks were systemized and the system followed.

We then set about identifying our target market. Once this was done, we concentrated on designing our marketing to appeal to those targets. We started collecting customer details and created a database that we could market to. We raised the bar on customer service and established the expectation of excellent service, and actively managed team membership around this expectation.

Everything was measured. The aim was to know the numbers every week—and by this I mean the number of tables, the number of diners, and average dollar sale. Every opportunity was taken to look for additional sales opportunities.

Testing and measuring played a vital role in transforming this business. All marketing efforts were tested and measured, and all procedures that didn't work were stopped. All marketing is now tested on a small scale, before it gets expensive. All business Key Performance Indicators—sales, average sale, number of diners, stock rollover and wastage, portion measuring—are all measured and monitored.

Since coaching began, sales are up 20 percent and customer numbers and the average dollar sale are consistently up on a weekly basis.

The team members are now more stable, and more productive. They have a greater focus on creating an exceptional dining experience for every customer, every time.

The owners now work four or five days per week only, and have time off together every week. They now have a life. And they are well on the way to having a manager who can run the business without them, for longer periods. The team is far more productive, happier, and stable. We are still improving the team every month, and we have a recruiting system that consistently delivers excellent prospects for them.

The kitchen is now essentially a self-sustaining, self-contained unit. Orders, cleaning, and kitchen activities are self-managed by the kitchen team. The owners don't need to continually supervise that area any longer.

The routine of ordering, daily team management, maintenance, and daily operations are almost at a point where the systems run the business.

The Outcome

Wendy and Cengiz are working towards having all these systems and the right people in place so they can concentrate on establishing a tourist business overseas. They're planning on spending at least three months away from the business soon, checking out various options. Longer term, they're either thinking of selling the restaurant or leasing it and settling overseas.

They say the best thing about working with a Coach has been the accountability that makes sure they do the work. "This would never have gotten done, I don't think, if Steve hadn't made us set goals and tasks, and actually achieve them," Wendy said. "It's gotten us into good habits whereas before, trying to get something done was a mammoth task, even if it was a little thing. So definitely, setting the goals and tasks and achieving them has been our biggest achievement."

Wendy recommends that every business owner should consider a Business Coach. "I would definitely recommend it. He has such a wealth of knowledge. And for someone like myself who hasn't had a lot to do with running a business before, I've learned quite a lot from him and have certainly benefited from it."

Part 5

▪ How to Implement Systems without Causing Mass Panic

Knowing what systems you need to implement is one thing, but knowing how to go about implementing them without causing your team to panic is another. And believe me, unless you go about it properly, you really do run the risk of causing your team to read too much into your actions.

It's an old belief that businesses automate to reduce the number of people they employ. This probably started when factories began introducing automated machinery to do more quickly and more efficiently what factory workers had previously been doing.

But it was not just on the factory floor that management found better ways of going about their business. In the office, the equivalent of the automated machine is the system, which achieves the same result through the elimination or minimization of human error, lapses of concentration, or oversights in judgment. It's the system that ensures that the business runs like clockwork day-in and day-out. It's the system that ensures that nothing is overlooked, left to chance, or forgotten about. And it's the system that ensures consistency in customer service, performance, and the day-to-day operation of the business.

Introducing new systems into your business will involve a lot more than just a detailed knowledge of your business, what systems it needs, and the results they will produce. It involves a whole raft of human relationship skills that can severely test even the most experienced and well-respected of managers.

You see, what you are dealing with here, apart from the technicalities of your business, is human nature, and we all know how fickle that can be.

The first thing you are going to need to do is to understand as much as you can about human nature. You are going to have to understand that all people are different; they have different needs and requirements, they fear different things, they have different views about job security, and different things motivate them.

But it's not just your team that you need to understand; you also need to understand yourself, both as a manager and as a person. You see, your team members look at you as their manager, and they expect you to behave in a certain way. It's how they perceive you that counts, not how you actually are as a person. You will probably see yourself one way, but your team will see a very different you.

So let's concentrate on understanding the different personality types of your team first, then we'll consider you as a manager.

The DISC Personality Profile

Everyone has weaknesses, and this system is meant as a guide to identify them. Remember, if you are happy as you are, that's great.

When you read the characteristics of the various personality types, you will start to understand how and why people can be expected to behave when you interact with them. Remember, with all knowledge should come wisdom. Knowing the best time and way to use this knowledge is what makes the difference.

High I Personalities

High I's like to have fun and be popular. You can recognise them by their outgoing and very friendly manner. They want to be friends with people. They will rarely tell anyone off. When they say something in anger, they don't want you to remind them of it again, because that was in the past and they really weren't that serious when they said it in the first place.

High I's don't like to get into too much detail, as they don't find that fun. They like to work with others in a changing environment. High I's can be recognized by their very friendly disposition. They look you in the eye and usually use a lot of tonal changes in their voices.

They talk a bit louder than other personality types, except the High D, who can also talk confidently and loudly. This is the mark of an extrovert. The difference between them is that High I's are loud and friendly. If you joke with either of them a High I will respond, but a High D may not.

High I's will respond quicker, because they think you're like them, so they'll let you know by giving you a friendly response.

High I Interaction

High I's get on fairly well with most personality types. They can annoy the High C's and High D's because they're task-oriented and just want to get the job done without being friendly while doing it. All the other personality types can see a High I as overly friendly. They might say, "Mellow out a bit. You come on too strong and annoy people. Don't be so friendly."

High I's are good motivators and team leaders, although they won't like pulling team members into line if they've done something they shouldn't have.

Introducing Systems with the High I

To manage High I's, you need to win them over and be their friend. If you don't show you care about them or that you like them, they won't want to work for you.

You need to show that you have a sense of humor, are a fun-loving person, and you are having fun talking to them right now. You can work on being a little bit stern, but not too serious.

High I's want to do what seems popular. They don't want to do anything that seems like detailed work that will take up lots of their time. If it seems boring to them, they won't want it. The best thing you can say to them is that it will be a lot of fun.

They will work well with people who seem to have the same nature as they do. So be happy and spontaneous. Talk about other things apart from work. Get chatty at the start, during the middle, and the end of the work process. They will sometimes want to go off on a tangent. Let them do most of the talking. They love to talk about anything, especially other people.

Be their friend and advise them on what you think and feel is best for them. Be sincere. Be like them and they will love you.

In terms of gaining support for a new system from High I's, there are a few things to remember. If you're a High D, don't talk too much. Let them decide that they want the system and that it seems like a popular idea and makes sense. High D's need to be more friendly than usual when they are in the workplace.

You can't be too friendly with High I's, as long as you're sincere. They are people's people and have great people skills. They won't like you if you act fake.

High I's are prone to exaggerate. They like to tell stories and you can too when working with them. But tell them if you are exaggerating.

Areas They Need to Work On

High I's need to work on getting the job done and not being distracted by other people. They need to be more task oriented. They need to get into the detail more, as this is what they don't like doing.

They need to be less extroverted with people, especially High C's and High S's. When communicating with High C's they don't need to be their friend, which is what they believe.

High I's are a bit too friendly for the High S's, although the High S's can see that aspect of them and not let it bother them. High I's need to recognise that the other personality types are not like them. They also need to work on being more like the others when communicating with them.

High D Personalities

High D's like to be in control. They want to be at the top and give the orders. They have a hard time following orders, as they feel that their own way is always better. High D's will usually end up in managment positions, self-employed, or in charge of a section that has a bit of room to move unsupervised.

They like to be in control of their own lives and make their own decisions. High D's can seem to be too powerful or too strong for other people. They are confident, outspoken, and say what they feel. This can offend others, as they can be thought of as arrogant. They aren't usually; it's just the way they express themselves.

High D's have active minds that like to be stimulated; they like to be doing lots of things at once. When they do more than one thing at a time the quality can start to drop. It can be difficult for them to follow something to its end. They feel a great need for lots of activity. When you want something done in a hurry, give it to a High D.

High D Interaction

High D's do not interact well with others. They give orders and like to take control, and this can detract from their relationships with others.

High D's can sabotage or undermine the authority of a High I and not be at all worried about it affecting their popularity. While the High I likes to have fun working with a group, the High D isn't that interested, or at least not to the same degree.

Often High D's have a lot of High I in them; they just need to tap into it a bit more to get on better with a High I.

High D's work well with High C's. Neither needs to be friendly while they work, so they get the job done. The two personalities compliment each other very well. The High D gets on best with a High C. A High D likes to delegate, and the best one to delegate to is the High C.

However, because the High D is not detail-oriented and the High C is, a problem can occur. The High C will need lots of details on how to do something, and this is precisely something the High D doesn't like to give.

Also High C's prefer to do the same thing over and over. They like doing the things they know how to do. That's often how they get their significance and feelings of importance; by doing something perfectly.

A High D gets along reasonably well with a High S because the latter is steadying, reserved, and tolerant of others. High S's don't need to be given the details like a High C does. They can just be told what to do and they do it.

High S's know that High D's like to control others and don't let it worry them. High D's don't consider their mode of interaction, like needing to relay instructions with details for the High C, or with friendliness to a High I, so the High S works best with a High D.

High D's may think the High S's are inferior because they mistake their natural reserve and steadiness with lacking in confidence. Often High S's have great self-confidence; they just don't need to display it like a High D does. High D's like confident people, as they can relate better to them.

Introducing Systems with a High D

High D's like to be leaders. They like to do what no one else is doing. They like to be innovative pioneers. The best way to work with them is to tell them that they need to be more productive, profitable, and successful. They need to become leaders of others.

Respect them and never make them feel inferior. They need to respect the manager. Most importantly, they need to be confident that you can deliver what you say you can. They need to be given the facts and reasons. Also don't try to be too friendly with them.

In terms of systems, they want a summary of its features. They don't need details; in fact going over details annoys them. Give a brief outline of different things showing the logic of it all. They want to be productive so telling them how the system can help them perform more efficiently will be helpful. Tell them that they will be more successful using the new system. That's what they want to know.

Give them better solutions or ways of doing things. Be blunt if you have to; they won't mind, but only if they have your respect.

Areas They Need to Work On

The major area they need to work on is their people skills and communication with others. They also need to slow down to check if they are making progress. When talking to a High C, they need to give more specifics.

They need to be friendlier with other team members. They need progress checks to see how well they are doing. Are the jobs they start being completed, and if so, how good is the quality? They need to stop, plan, and think more before they start, and also as they progress.

High S Personalities

High S's are steady people. They don't like to rush things. When everyone else is stressing out, they remain calm. They like to plod along, thinking things over before doing anything. They don't like making quick decisions.

They are well liked by all personality types because they are friendly, easy-going, and harmless. People admire their cool disposition. They just get in and get the job done, although usually not at a great pace.

While High D's start going flat out without knowing if they are doing it right, the High I gets everyone together so they can all get involved and have fun. The High C plans every detail meticulously before making a start, while the High S thinks it over for quite a while before making a slow start.

High S Interaction

High S's get on well with High D's because they probably understand them, and it doesn't worry them when the High D gives orders. Because High S's are calm, they are a help to the High D.

High S's can plan things, which is a help to the High D. They slow the High D down, and this can be a good or a bad thing. High D's often end up marrying High S's.

The High S gets along well with the High I. They are both people oriented. The High S is a calmer, more reserved version of the High I. While the High I will respond, "Get a bit more life in you."

They both have fun in life, or try to. The High S has a high concern for others and tries to understand them. When High I's work with High S's, they can often get carried away with having fun, as they're not as task-oriented as the High D and the High C.

The two usually won't get as much done as the other two personality types.

High S's and High C's are both introverted. They both like to take their time in making a decision. They work well together, although they won't get a task done as quickly as the D's and I's. They will think about it for a while first.

The High S will feel there's no need to rush into it. The High C's will agree because they will want to consider all the details before they start anyway. The High C's will be planning it out perfectly before they start, and if it's taking too long to start, the High S's won't say too much because they like to keep the peace.

However the two personality types will get a job done well together and it will be done correctly.

The High D and High S complement each other nicely. The High S will bring the High D's feet back down to earth and steady them. The High D will speed up the High S's decision-making process, which is sometimes needed.

The High S admires the High D's leadership ability, while the High D admires the High S's steadiness. Because the High S's are reserved while the High D's are outgoing, they learn from each other in different situations.

Introducing Systems with a High S

They are harder to work with than the High D or I. They like to be steady in their decision making. They don't like to rush anything. They like to take their time in reaching a decision. They don't like pressure or pushy people.

You need to be their friend and build genuine rapport with them. Be reserved like they are. Be casual. Give them data to make a decision and tell them when you will be phasing in new processes.

Be reserved like they are. The High S's don't like change, so tell them that the new system won't involve any major changes. Tell them it's a nice slow process.

Give them plenty of eye contact. Build rapport and be their friend.

Areas They Need to Work On

High S's need to work on changing their ways more quickly. They change in time; however, they are the most reluctant of all personality types to do so. High D's will change before you finish telling them why they need to. To High I's change is fun. They like change because they like variety in their lives.

High C's won't usually change much at all. This is because they have just finished learning how to do something the best way they can, and now they just want to keep doing it. They love getting into a routine. How can you achieve perfection in anything if you don't stick to it for ages?

High S's need to practice making quick decisions. They need to realize that often a quick decision is better than no decision at all.

High C Personalities

High C's are interesting in many ways. They have a tendency to collect data, facts, and figures. They can often stutter their words when describing things, possibly due to tension, and also because they are thinking what the perfect way to describe this is. High C's often stutter more than other personality types.

High C's like to do things very well, if not perfectly. However, they don't reference their standards to others, which would be valuable to them because then they would learn that their standards are much higher than everyone else's.

They often create stress in their lives by this ongoing quest to live up to their own perfect standards. They can miss out on seeing the big picture as they can get stuck on the details.

They want to work on their own because they feel that they will do the job best. They think that other people won't do as good a job as they will. High C's are reserved and task-oriented, which means they aren't that friendly in communication with other people, especially nonfamily and friends.

They like to give lots of data when they communicate, as they feel this is what people want.

They can have high levels of stress due to rarely being able to live up to their own high standards. They like to have many details before making a decision. They virtually never rush into anything, especially without considering all the facts, data, and graphs. Then they like to think more on it.

They don't like to be pushed into doing things, as they feel that their way is nearly always the best. They like to plan things out before lifting a finger. Conditions usually have to be perfect before they proceed.

Bradley J. Sugars

High C Interaction

High C's compliment High D's because they are virtual opposites; one is introverted and the other is extroverted. The High C is reserved while the High D is outgoing. Both are task oriented.

High C's get self-satisfaction and pride from doing things for others. Although if they don't know how to do what the High D is asking, there can be problems.

The High C needs to be shown in detail how to do something. The High D isn't into details, so a communication problem can occur. For this pairing to work, the High D's need to explain in more detail how to do the things they want done.

A High C and a High I are an interesting combination. They can work well together, although they can often have troubles. When they struggle in relationships, it can be due to their opposite natures. A High I is extroverted, while a High C is introverted.

A High I person is people oriented while a High C is task oriented. These traits can cause a lot of conflict. The High I will say or think that the High C is spending too much time on unimportant things. The High C may think the High I is flaky and doesn't work on what is really important.

The High C will want the High I to be less friendly and more task oriented, while the High I will think the opposite.

As a working combination, the two are good for each other if they can put aside their differences. The High I's will stop the High C's from being introverted and get them to have more fun and work with others. The High C's will bring the High I's back down to earth and get them working on the details. As a combination in business, they can work well together.

Introducing Systems with a High C

Introducing systems with a High C can be challenging. High C's can be very skeptical of anyone who says they have something they'll need because they often feel that what they already have is good.

They can resist change because they have their own way of doing things. They

84

won't consider accepting a new system unless the facts (of which there must be lots) are shown as valid.

Be prepared to spend a lot of time with them. They will ask a hundred questions and procrastinate because they will be wondering whether they've covered every detail they need to know about.

They will be wary of change agents. This is mainly because they have found how to do things without anyone's help, and a new system will mean that they'll need to relearn. They're much happier doing what they already know how to do.

They aren't overly friendly like the High I and High S. You can't just tell them that they need your system like you can the High D. They want only one thing—data. So give them as much data as you can. And give it in graph form, table form, written form, or essay form.

You can't give High C's too much data to consider. They like to justify their decisions by logic. They don't care if you are their best friend. They always consider the facts first.

Don't expect High C's to make quick decisions. They like time to think. So give it to them. Talk about facts backed up by logic. Get back to them another day only if you tell them you've given them everything they need to make a decision.

They are confident in their own abilities and are used to relying on making their own decisions. They will talk confidently because they have a lot of knowledge and are proud of it. If you tell them you have a way of helping them do things better and more efficiently, you will get their attention eventually. Anything that improves their standards or efficiency they will love. Tell them they'll be able to do even better with this.

Areas They Need to Work On

Their own standards can be too high compared to others. They can be stressed people due to feeling that everything they do needs to be perfect. This is the standard they always strive for.

They need to get other people's opinions when working on a task and accept their standards as being good enough. A High C needs to strive for excellence, not perfection!

Most High C's think they can do a better job, and often they can. But usually the standard a High C works to is too high because everyone else acknowledges excellence, while a High C keeps on chasing perfection. High C's need to stop at excellence.

They need to work more with others to get used to their level of excellence, and then to accept it as their own *new* standard.

High C's need to be more confident in their approach to decision making and not fear arriving at a wrong decision. After all, High D's make decisions a lot more quickly than a High C ever will. High D's far outweigh High C's when it comes to successful people. So, High C's need to get into the habit of making quicker decisions so they can develop a better, stronger, emotional muscle.

High C's need to do things that are new or different. They need to forget their schedules. Throw them away for a day. Do something spontaneous. Do something on the spur of the moment. Do something because it looks like fun. They need to tell themselves that change is fun, that it is good.

They also need to get more help from others. They need to ask themselves if what they are doing is the most important thing they could be doing. Will spending the time doing it perfectly really benefit them or others, or should they say, "This is excellent. What can I do next?"

High C's need to move on more. They need to get more involved with people. They need to open up and tell others what they are feeling. A very wise man once said, "Vulnerability is strength because you open yourself up to change and improvement."

They need to take on more like a High D does. They need to do more things at once so they don't get stuck on the details that aren't always important.

People under Pressure

To better understand this section, remember the four main personality types: D—Dominant, I—Influential, S—Steady, and C—Compliant.

People can change their natures under pressure. High I's can become High S's under pressure. This means that they slow down and think more; they become more reserved.

High I's can become High D's, which means instead of being friendly to everyone, they start to boss everyone around without much regard for their feelings. People around them would wonder what happened to that friendly person who got on with everyone so well.

High D's can become High C's under pressure. They will now consider details and think carefully before making a decision. High D's could go to High S's, meaning they will steady themselves and slow down. They will consider the people around them more.

High S's could even become High D's under pressure. They now have to act and think quickly when placed under lots of pressure. They might start to become loud and bark out orders when normally they are calm, reserved, and friendly.

High C's could move to High D's under pressure. They will think and act more quickly than previously, making decisions quickly and not consider all the details. You've heard people say they work best under pressure; this could mean that they've become High D's under pressure to get more done.

Normally a High C wouldn't change to a High I or High S under pressure, or a High I wouldn't go to a High C under pressure, as these two personality types are so different.

Often a person stays the same under pressure. A High D can stay a High D. A High S can stay a High S, and so on. Not everyone changes under pressure. You will know when someone does. It will be quite noticeable.

Different Styles of Leadership

By now you will have realized that you need to tailor the way you interact with your team members to suit their individual personality types. This will help you achieve the best results when implementing new systems into your business.

You have to adapt your leadership style to suit the situation you are dealing with.

You need to understand the various styles of leadership before you can decide which one is best when introducing new systems. And that will have a lot to do with the types of personalities you have working for you.

So what are the different styles of leadership?

Consider first the two basic types of leader. I'm talking in general terms here. What two stereotypes spring immediately to mind?

Most people will say the tough, no-nonsense type and the easygoing type. And they would be right.

I'm sure that you will have come across examples of these two styles. We all know what type Army Sergeant Majors are!

What style applies to you? No, I don't mean what style do you *think* you are. I mean what style are you in the eyes of your team. There is a difference here—a huge difference—because it really doesn't matter what you think; it's what your team thinks that counts. You might very well be a caring, easygoing type at home, but if your team doesn't perceive this, it's irrelevant. It's how you are as a leader in your team members' eyes that will affect their behavior. Do you know what type of leader they think you are?

The first dimension along which leadership style is defined ranges from *democratic* to *autocratic*. The democratic leader is one who involves others in the leadership decision-making process, whereas the autocratic leader doesn't. Most leaders fall somewhere in the middle of these two extremes. They fall somewhere along the democratic-autocratic scale.

Of course, this is a simplistic view of leadership style. Life isn't so clear-cut. What other major characteristics could we use to identify leadership styles? This other dimension characterizes leadership styles according to the degree to which they concentrate on task behavior or relationship behavior.

What does this mean?

When a leader gets involved with team members, telling them exactly what to do and when, how to do it, and where it should be done, that's a good example of task behavior. The main concern here of the leader is getting the job done.

Relationship behavior, on the other hand, has more to do with explaining, listening, encouraging, supporting, and generally facilitating team members when they go about tackling their tasks. Can you see the difference?

You can illustrate leadership styles by considering the four types together. They can also be graphically explained by means of the following diagram:

	High Relationship and Low Task **3**	High Relationship and High Task **2**
	Low Relationship and Low Task **4**	Low Relationship and High Task **1**

(Left vertical axis, bottom to top): (Low) ----------- Relationship Behavior ----------- (High)
Providing Supportive Behavior

(Bottom axis): (Low) --------------- Task Behavior --------------- (High)
Providing Directive Behavior

From this you can see that some managers will concentrate on task-related behavior and not on relationship behavior (Style 1) while those characterised as Style 2 will display high task and relationship behaviors. Style 3 leaders display high relationship behavior and low task behavior, while Style 4 leaders are low in both task and relationship behavior.

Understand that there are no right or wrong leadership styles. You don't have to set about changing your style just because you might be a Style 4 person. There is a place for all styles. Consider the situation where you have really efficient, experienced salespeople whom you can rely on at all times. In this case Style 4 would be totally appropriate, wouldn't it? Interfering too much (by adopting a

Style 1 approach, for instance) would prove counterproductive as your salespeople would feel you no longer trust the standard of work they were performing. They'd feel you were interfering in their jobs, wouldn't they?

The important point here is that you should adapt your leadership style to suit not only the current situation, but also the situation as it evolves. You might, for instance, use a Style 1 approach when starting a new business, then switching to Style 2 as the business establishes itself. You see, your team members will have become a lot more confident and comfortable in their jobs, but they would still require a high level of task behavior input from you. They will then be needing more relationship behavior input, which means more emotional support, positive feedback, and encouragement. Then as they become proficient in their jobs, they will appreciate being allowed to *run their own shows* without interference. However, they will still require a high level of relationship behavior input from you. This will do wonders for their confidence levels, which in turn will produce results for your bottom line. Finally, Style 4 will be appropriate when your business and your team members could be considered mature. They will need little in the way of supportive behavior from you. A good example of this situation is when the owner of the business has stepped aside, allowing the business to run itself.

The leader needs to assess the situation and bring the appropriate style to the situation. If you had a mature business in which you generally employed a Style 4 type of leadership, and you now wanted to introduce systems to run the business, you'd probably change to a Style 2 for the duration of the installation process. Then change to a Style 3 while the team members get used to the systems, then finally back to a Style 4 once they have been properly installed and tested, as well as making sure the team members are totally comfortable with the new process.

Communication Is the Key

Many regard communication to be the lifeblood of business, and I would tend to agree. Effective communication is a two-way process that leads to understanding. Does your team really understand what you are trying to achieve? Do they really understand how the new systems will benefit them? And do you really understand their fears or concerns? Or do you just *think* they do?

Understand that your ability to effectively communicate with your team members depends on their willingness to let you communicate to them. As I said earlier, it is a two-way process; it takes two to tango.

One of the factors that will determine whether your team members will allow you to effectively communicate with them is their level of readiness. Another is the level of influence you have over them. To gauge this you need to first consider the type of power you have in your business. Is it largely based on the position you hold there, or is it personal power? You need to give some thought to the relationship between your style of leadership and the type of power you enjoy. The two must be interrelated; otherwise you won't be effective. For instance, positional power can underpin Styles 1 and 2, whereas personal power is more appropriate when using Styles 3 and 4.

Very often it is expeditious to bring in change agents or business coaches to assist in the process of installing systems, particularly in cases where positional power is required. They can get the job done without being distracted by relationship issues.

Is this appropriate for your business?

But whatever approach you feel suits your situation, you simply must communicate well with your team members every step along the way. Involve them in the process and enlist their help from the very beginning. Let them have a significant input, as this will not only help them to *buy into* the whole process by giving them ownership, it will also prove beneficial because they know their areas of the business better than anyone else. Remember, they are the experts as far as their jobs are concerned.

Another benefit of thorough communication is that your team members will begin to see and appreciate the benefits of the system. They will realize what's in it for them.

Plan Well

Systems are orderly things out of necessity. But when implementing systems into a business, it's more than just the systems themselves that have to be orderly. The entire process itself has to be conducted in an orderly fashion.

It all starts in your mind. From the time you initially think up the reasoning for introducing systems, through the design of the individual systems, and during the actual implementation process itself, order is the name of the game.

This calls for a clear mind and meticulous planning.

Think things through carefully; don't rush at it like a bull in a china shop. Make use of planning aids like flowcharts, and use them to outline the process to your team. Build in opportunities to celebrate your milestones. Whenever a milestone is reached, throw a party, give out awards of recognition, or give those involved time off. Do whatever you have to do to make the process enjoyable, fun, and nonthreatening. Make use of a progress chart so that your team members can see their progress and how they are achieving their goals.

Involve Your Team

Make sure you *really* involve everyone who has an interest in the new systems. This mustn't be token involvement, but meaningful involvement. Encourage your team members to keep an eye out for shortcomings in the newly introduced systems. Understand that they will become your systems experts in no time at all because they will be the ones living with them.

Encourage them to develop or suggest improvements to the systems. You'll be surprised at how much your team members will get to know about the intricate workings of the system. Give them the go-ahead to make suggestions, because over time, things will change, which means the systems will need updating. This is only natural and not an indication of any inherent weaknesses in your systems. You see, your operating environment will almost certainly change over time, and this will necessitate changes in the way you operate.

Don't forget to tie in your KPIs with the introduction of systems. This will encourage them to make sure they meet prescribed performance standards during the implementation process. It will also ensure they receive appropriate rewards for their efforts. Do this and you will be going a long way towards ensuring that your implementation process progresses smoothly and without mass panic.

Part 6

■ How to Extricate Yourself from the Business and Hand Over Your Duties

In many ways, this is the hardest part of the whole process. This is because, until now, what you'll have been doing is designing, planning, and implementing systems to run your business. These are all work-related tasks that will be familiar to you. They involve skills and behaviours that are in keeping with your position in your business.

What you'll be doing now is effecting a massive change in your mindset. You see, you'll be making a change from basically having a job in your business to becoming semiretired.

And that's not all that will be changing. In addition to your relationship with the members of your team, your relationship with money will be changing. Whereas in the past you will have been making money by taking a wage from the business, you will in future start getting profit.

You will need to learn how to let go of the business. Your whole relationship with the business will change. But unless you handle this entire process carefully, it can backfire and leave you with a mess.

So how do you ensure that this doesn't happen? How do you ensure that the transition is smooth and that the business is able to operate successfully and profitably without you?

Create the Right Environment

Before you begin implementing change within your business, you need to ensure that the environment for change is right. It's no use expecting things to go the way you hope if the conditions are not right.

Ideally, you want the members of your team to say, "Yes, now is the time to introduce the new system. We simply can't continue the way we have been in the past. The market has changed and unless we do too, we will be left behind. Then my livelihood will be at stake."

The environment also needs to be perfect in another way too. There needs to be a climate of trust in your business, because you will be asking your team members to step outside their comfort zones by putting their faith in new and as yet untried (as far as they are concerned) ways of going about their daily tasks. You will be expecting them to trust your judgment. They will also realize that you have to trust their abilities to implement, operate, and rely on the new systems.

Open Communication Channels

One of the key factors to ensuring the right environment for change is having open communication channels. It is vital that you are able to communicate with your team and vice versa. This is where an *open door* policy can be useful.

Of course, it's not just the physical aspect of communication I am talking about here; I'm talking about the need for *effective* communication.

What does this mean? It means that the messages being communicated are actually *understood*. Understand that this does not only imply that the messages are received and literally understood; it means that the *content* and the *intention* is understood. It also means that the messages are *acted upon*, if necessary. You see, the communication must result in some sort of *action*.

If these conditions are met, then your team will have confidence in you and your ability to work *on* the business and not *in* it. It will also make a major contribution towards ensuring that the environment is right for the implementation of systems in your business.

Provide Continuous Feedback

One of the risks that has to be minimized during a process such as this is the change process's developing a mind of its own and going off in an unwanted direction.

This can happen through weak leadership. To counter this, you need to ensure that you employ the appropriate leadership style and that you keep strictly to your plan and schedule.

The easiest and most effective way of doing this is by providing your team members with constant feedback.

Keep them up-to-date with developments. Let them know how they are doing. Give them encouragement and let them know that they have your support. And encourage them to supply you with feedback as well. Remember, effective communication is a two-way street. And remember too that communication is the lifeblood of any business. So don't neglect your communication strategies. Make them a priority.

Involve the Entire Team

One of the biggest mistakes you can make is to involve a select few in the systemization of your business. Avoid the temptation to appoint an implementation team, as it will only lead to fragmentation, frustration, and discontent.

Involve all team members, as it is vitally important that they take ownership of the entire process. You see, this way you will not only stand a far better chance of the systems being introduced and implemented effectively and efficiently, but you'll be making a major contribution to your next goal as well, that of being able to extricate yourself from the business.

You'll be taking the first definite steps on the way to letting go of your business, of handing over the reins to those who will ultimately be responsible for ensuring that you are able to enjoy a real passive income—the entire team.

Give Them Responsibility

It's no use expecting your team to do all the hard work and to put their necks on the line without giving them true responsibility for their jobs and their actions. That would be like tying one hand behind a boxer's back and still expecting him to win his bout in the ring.

If your team members are accountable for their functions, give them the responsibility to go with it.

And give them the rewards based on the results. This can, of course, take many forms. How about a share of the profits?

You'll be surprised at how well even the most junior member of your team will perform if you hand over responsibility along with accountability.

Delegate

Being able to delegate is the hallmark of a true leader. It's also a sign that you have *come of age* in the business world.

Delegating work means more than just handing out tasks to individuals in your business; it means handing over the function lock, stock, and barrel. It means learning to let go and not wanting to do everything yourself.

How good are you at delegating? Can you trust your team members to do the job without making a hash of things? Can you sleep at night knowing that someone else is taking care of things that you previously prided yourself in doing? Do you shudder at the thought of stepping back and trusting your team to get on with things?

Being able to even contemplate stepping back from your business requires a quantum shift in your mindset. Yet if you really want to make progress in the world of business, it's something you have to do. You see, unless you do, you will find yourself forever tied to your business, slaving away unnecessarily instead of freeing yourself up so you can work *on* your business instead of *in* it. Without delegating, you'll never have the time to really get out and hunt for the fantastic opportunities that are waiting for you. Unless you do, you will never make real progress in building substantial wealth for yourself and your business. You'll never progress much further than owning a job. To find out more about this, read my book *Billionaire In Training*.

Hands Off

If you're serious about extricating yourself from your business, then the first thing you need to do is to appoint a general manager to run the business for you. Once you have done this, stepping back becomes really easy. This is because you'll now have someone there to run the show for you. You'll have no reason to be there any more.

Think of it this way: The general manager you hire is the expert at running a business, so let her get on with the job you hired her to do. The same goes for the other members of your team. They are the best people you could find to fill their positions at the time you were hiring, weren't they? So don't interfere with them. Leave them to get on with what you hired them to do in the first place. If you pursue this way of thinking (and it is the correct way), then you'll come to the conclusion that you have no place in your own business. You shouldn't be there. You will have no option but to take a *hands off* approach to business.

But there's one other thing you'll need to learn. And if you are like the vast majority of business owners I've dealt with, you'll need to learn to *trust*. That's right, you'll have to trust that the business will power along without your having to be there.

Can you see that everything we've discussed until now is all interlinked? Building the right environment, establishing good lines of communication, involving your team members in the decision-making process, letting them take ownership of the systemization process, and giving them true accountability and responsibility are all linked to the fact that you need to delegate and let go. They are all interlinked; each step relies on the others because, if one isn't implemented, the conditions won't be right for the others to be implemented properly.

Ease Yourself Out

Here are my tips for making your exit from your business as pain free as possible:

- Don't interfere with your team members or the work they are doing. You hired them to do the job, so let them get on with it.

- Give up your office and parking space. If you don't have an office to go to, you won't show up, as you'll soon start to feel uncomfortable hanging around the office like a spare part.

- Don't attend regular or routine meetings. Get your general manager to brief you by phone or e-mail afterwards.

- Keep your lines of communication open and remain accessible.

- Drop in from time to time or when needed.

Continue to Provide Support and Feedback

Running a business at this level requires a fine balance between maintaining an active interest in the affairs of the business and letting go of the day-to-day operational functions of the business. You wouldn't want to disappear into the wild blue yonder, but on the other hand, you don't want to become the proverbial pest that never stops interfering.

Your team members will appreciate hearing from you on a regular basis, especially if you continue to show support and appreciation for their efforts. This will show them that you are in touch with the business, even though you are allowing them to get on with running the business. They will begin to value you all the more for this, and their respect for you will grow enormously. They will see this as the sign of a true leader.

You too will benefit enormously, having the time to do the really important things you've always wanted to do. Yet from a personal point of view, you'll actually find yourself in semiretirement, at least as far as your working life is concerned.

Handling Semiretirement

Handling semiretirement presents a whole new set of challenges, especially to the busy business owner. There are many psychological factors to take into account, and there are many pitfalls to avoid. You see, until semiretirement everything had rested on your shoulders—everything had depended on you; this is no longer the case.

It's funny how most people spend their entire working lives dreaming of the day when they *wouldn't* have to go to work to get paid, yet when the time comes, most find this extremely difficult to deal with. The feelings of inadequacy and no longer being of use are very difficult to deal with, unless you change your formula for success.

You can spend time developing your social life now that you no longer have to trade time for money. You can spend time finding new friends and joining a whole new social circle. You will slowly but surely find, as you work at it, that it will become easier to let go of the business, particularly from an operational point of view. If you can't, you might just be sabotaging all you've achieved in business so far.

As your level of financial security improves—and it should have dramatically by now—you'll find you actually stop spending. I know this may sound strange, but believe me, you'll find that there just isn't anything more you need to buy. You see, by now you will have enough toys: cars, computers, cameras, television sets, hobbies, you name it. You'll have it all by now, and more.

Your lifestyle will have changed beyond your wildest dreams, and after a while you'll find yourself looking for fresh challenges.

Suddenly you'll discover the motivation to strive further.

And this won't involve going back *into* your business to begin working all over again; it will involve *investing* in the true sense of the word.

By now, you'll have begun setting yourself new business and personal goals. You will have seen the potential for duplicating what you have done in your first business and will realize how easy it is to do again. If it worked once for you, do you think it will work again? Of course it will. Why reinvent the wheel? After all, it's much simpler to use the same systems again and again.

You see, what you will be aiming at now is to *make money with money* to create *wealth*. Understand that you used to make money with time, but now you make it with other people's time and by having your money make money. The name of the game is to find a company that isn't performing anywhere near its true potential, buy it at a rock bottom price, build it up quickly using all the knowledge, skills, and systems you have learned or developed, and then to sell it for a premium price.

Finding these opportunities will be a whole new challenge and something you will relish. And you'll have the time on your hands to do this, as you will have successfully extricated yourself from your business. Are you beginning to see the real advantages of going down this path?

You might come across new opportunities through your business or social networks, or you might find them by just being observant. Some might advertise the fact they are looking for a new owner, while others still might approach you directly.

A surefire indicator that you're ready for your next challenge is when you begin feeling uncomfortable again. When you're itching for a new challenge. When it dawns on you that you're not the king anymore.

"Why should I move—it's harder?" you might aask. Well, yes and no. You see, the higher up the ladder you climb, the more *fun* it gets. Also, you won't be *working* harder, just *playing* for bigger stakes. And you'll be well on your way to getting *richer*.

▮ Conclusion

So there you have it—everything you need to know about systemizing your business.

Systemizing your business is important for a number of reasons. First it ensures that your business runs smoothly and consistently all the time, and second it frees you up, allowing you to spend your time far more lucratively and productively.

Once you've worked your way through this book, you'll know how to identify areas within your business to systemize and how to develop and write systems. You'll also know the four key areas of your business to systemize as well as the nine steps that are involved in the systemization process. This book will have shown you how to go about implementing systems without causing the members of your team to panic and jump ship. You'll also know everything you need to know about how to extricate yourself from the business so you can pursue other ventures.

What's more, systemizing your business will leave you with a team that's really empowered and committed to the business because they will, probably for the first time, be experiencing real job satisfaction. And they'll begin to regard you as a true leader.

So what are you waiting for? It's time to get into *Action*.

▌Getting into *Action*

So, when is the best time to start?

Now—right now—so let me give you a step-by-step method to get yourself onto the same success path of many of my clients and the clients of my team at **ActionCOACH.**

Start testing and measuring now.

You'll want to ask your customers and prospects how they found out about you and your business. This will give you an idea of what's been working and what hasn't. You also want to concentrate on the five areas of the business chassis. Remember:

1. Number of Leads from each campaign.
2. Conversion Rate from each and every campaign.
3. Number of Transactions on average per year per customer.
4. Average Dollar Sale from each campaign.
5. Your Margins on each product or service.

The Number of Leads is easy; just take a measure for four weeks, average it out, and multiply by 50 working weeks of the year. Of course you'd ask each lead where they came from so you've got enough information to make advertising decisions.

The Conversion Rate is a little trickier, not because it's hard to measure, but because we want to know a few more details. You want to know what level of conversion you have from each and every type of marketing strategy you use. Remember that some customers won't buy right away, so keep accurate records on each and every lead.

To find the Number of Transactions you'll need to go through your records. Hopefully you can find the transaction history of at least 50 of your past customers and then average out their yearly purchases.

The Average Dollar Sale is as simple as it sounds. The total dollars sold divided by the number of sales. The best information you can collect is the average from each marketing campaign you run, so that you know where the real profit is coming from.

And, of course, your margins. An Average Margin is good to know and measure, but to know the margins on everything you sell is the most powerful knowledge you can collect.

If you're having any challenges with your testing and measuring, be sure to contact your nearest **ActionCOACH** Business Coach. She'll be able to help you through and show you the specialized documents to use.

If, by chance, you're thinking of racing ahead before you test and measure, remember this. It's impossible to improve a score when you don't know what the score is.

So you've got your starting point. You know exactly what's going on in your business right now. In fact, you know more about not only what's happening right now, but also the factors that are going to create what will happen tomorrow.

The next step in your business growth is simple.

Let's decide what you want out of the business—in other words, your goals. Here are the main points I want you to plan for.

How many hours do you want to work each week? How much money do you want to take out of the business each month? And, most importantly, when do you want to finish the business?

By "finish" the business, I mean when it will be systematized enough so it can run without your having to be there. Remember this about business; a little bit of planning goes a long way, but to make a plan you have to have a destination.

Once again, if you're having difficulty, talk to an **ActionCOACH** Business Coach. He'll know exactly how to help you find what it is you really want out of both your business and your life.

Now the real work begins.

Remember, our goal is to get a 10 percent increase in each area over the next 12 months. Choose well, but I want to warn you of one thing, one thing I can literally guarantee.

Eight out of 10 marketing campaigns you run *will not work.*

That's why when you choose to run, say, an advertising campaign in your local newspaper, you've got to run at least 10 different ads. When you select a direct mail campaign, you should send out at least 10 different letters to test, and so on.

Make sure you get at least five strategies under each heading and plan to run at least one, preferably two, at least each month for the next 12 months.

Don't work on just one of the five areas at a time; mix it up a little so you get the synergy of all five areas working together.

Now, this is the most important advice I can give you:

Learn how to make each and every strategy work. Don't just think you know what to do; go through my hints and tips, read more books, listen to as many tapes as you can, watch all the videos you can find, talk to the experts, and make sure you get the most advantage you can before you invest a whole lot of money.

The next 12 months are going to be a matter of doing the numbers, running the campaigns, testing headlines, testing offers, testing prices, and, of course, measuring the results.

By the end of it you should have at least five new strategies in each of the five areas working together to produce a great result.

Once again I want to stress that this will work and this will make your business grow as long as *you* work it.

Is it simple? *Yes.*

Is it easy? *No.*

You'll have to work hard. If you can get the guidance of someone who's been there before you, then get it.

Whatever you do, start it now, start it today, and most importantly, make the most of every day. Your past does not equal your future; you decide your future right here and right now.

Be who you want to be, *do* what you need to do, in order to *have* what you want to have.

Positive *thought* without positive **ActionCOACH** leaves you with positively *nothing*. I called my company **ActionCOACH** for this very reason.

So take the first step—and get into *Action*.

■ ABOUT THE AUTHOR

Bradley J. Sugars

Brad Sugars is a world-renowned Australian entrepreneur, author, and business coach who has helped more than a million clients around the world find business and personal success.

He's a trained accountant, but as he puts it, most of his experience comes from owning his own companies. Brad's been in business for himself since age 15 in some way or another, although his father would argue he started at 7 when he was caught selling his Christmas presents to his brothers. He's owned and operated more than two dozen companies, from pizza to ladies fashion, from real estate to insurance and many more.

His main company, **ActionCOACH,** started from humble beginnings in the back bedroom of a suburban home in 1993 when Brad started teaching business owners how to grow their sales and marketing results. Now **ActionCOACH** has over 1000 franchises in 26 countries and is ranked in the top 100 franchises in the world.

Brad Sugars has spoken on stage with the likes of Tom Hopkins, Brian Tracy, John Maxwell, Robert Kiyosaki, and Allen Pease, written books with people like Anthony Robbins, Jim Rohn, and Mark Victor Hansen, appeared on countless TV and radio programs and in literally hundreds of print articles around the globe. He's been voted as one of the Most Admired Entrepreneurs by the readers of *E-Spy* magazine—next to the likes of Rupert Murdoch, Henry Ford, Richard Branson, and Anita Roddick.

Today, **ActionCOACH** has coaches across the globe and is ranked as one of the Top 25 Fastest Growing Franchises on the planet as well as the #1 Business Consulting Franchise. The success of **ActionCOACH** is simply attributed to the fact that they apply the strategies their coaches use with business owners.

Brad is a proud father and husband, the chairman of a major children's charity, and in his own words, "a very average golfer."

Check out Brad's Web site www.bradsugars.com and read the literally hundreds of testimonials from those who've gone before you.

■ RECOMMENDED READING LIST

ACTIONCOACH BOOK LIST

"The only difference between *you* now and *you* in 5 years' time will be the people you meet and the books you read." Charlie Tremendous Jones

"And, the only difference between *your* income now and *your* income in 5 years' time will be the people you meet, the books you read, the tapes you listen to, and then how *you* apply it all." Brad Sugars

- Brad Sugars "MindRICH" 3-hour Video
- Leverage—Board Game by Brad Sugars
- Action Speaks Louder than Words and 6 Steps to a Better Business CD or DVD. FREE OF CHARGE to Business Owners
- *The E-Myth Revisited* by Michael E. Gerber
- *My Life in Advertising & Scientific Advertising* by Claude Hopkins
- *Tested Advertising Methods* by John Caples
- *Building the Happiness Centered Business* by Dr. Paddi Lund
- *Write Language* by Paul Dunn & Alan Pease
- *7 Habits of Highly Effective People* by Steven Covey
- *First Things First* by Steven Covey
- *Awaken the Giant Within* by Anthony Robbins
- *Unlimited Power* by Anthony Robbins
- *22 Immutable Laws of Marketing* by Al Ries & Jack Trout
- *21 Ways to Increase Your Advertising Response* by Mark Tier
- *The One Minute Salesperson* by Spencer Johnson & Larry Wilson
- *The One Minute Manager* by Spencer Johnson & Kenneth Blanchard
- *The Great Sales Book* by Jack Collis
- *Way of the Peaceful Warrior* by Dan Millman

*To order Brad Sugars' products from the recommended reading list, call your nearest ActionCOACH office today.

■ The 18 Most Asked Questions about Working with an ActionCOACH Business Coach

And 18 great reasons why you'll jump at the chance to get your business flying and make your dreams come true

1. So who is ActionCOACH?

ActionCOACH is a business Coaching and Consulting company started in 1993 by entrepreneur and author Brad Sugars. With offices around the globe and business coaches from Singapore to Sydney to San Francisco, **ActionCOACH** has been set up with you, the business owner, in mind.

Unlike traditional consulting firms, **ActionCOACH** is designed to give you both short-term assistance and long-term training through its affordable Mentoring approach. After 14 years teaching business owners how to succeed, **ActionCOACH**'s more than 10,000 clients and 1,000,000 seminar attendees will attest to the power of the programs.

Based on the sales, marketing, and business management systems created by Brad Sugars, your **ActionCOACH** is trained to not only show you how to increase your business revenues and profits, but also how to develop the business so that you as the owner work less and relax more.

ActionCOACH is a franchised company, so your local **ActionCOACH** is a fellow business owner who's invested her own time, money, and energy to make her business succeed. At **ActionCOACH,** your success truly does determine our success.

2. And, why do I need a Business Coach?

Every great sports star, business person, and superstar is surrounded by coaches and advisors.

And, as the world of business moves faster and gets more competitive, it's difficult to keep up with both the changes in your industry and the innovations in sales, marketing, and management strategies. Having a business coach is no longer a luxury; it's become a necessity.

On top of all that, it's impossible to get an objective answer from yourself. Don't get me wrong. You can survive in business without the help of a Coach, but it's almost impossible to thrive.

A Coach *can* see the forest for the trees. A Coach will make you focus on the game. A Coach will make you run more laps than you feel like. A Coach will tell it like it is. A Coach will give you small pointers. A Coach will listen. A Coach will be your marketing manager, your sales director, your training coordinator, your partner, your confidant, your mentor, your best friend, and an *Action* Business Coach will help you make your dreams come true.

3. Then, what's an Alignment Consultation?

Great question. It's where an *Action* Coach starts with every business owner. You'll invest a minimum of $1295, and during the initial 2 to 3 hours your Coach invests with you, he'll learn as much as he can about your business, your goals, your challenges, your sales, your marketing, your finances, and so much more.

All with three goals in mind: To know exactly where your business is now. To clarify your goals both in the business and personally. And thirdly, to get the crucial pieces of information he needs to create your businesses *Action* Plan for the next 12 months.

Not a traditional business or marketing plan mind you, but a step-by-step plan of *Action* that you'll work through as you continue with the Mentor Program.

4. So, what, then, is the Mentor Program?

Simply put, it's where your *Action* Coach will work with you for a full 12 months to make your goals a reality. From weekly coaching calls and goal-setting sessions, to creating marketing pieces together, you will develop new sales strategies and business systems so you can work less and learn all that you need to know about how to make your dreams come true.

You'll invest between $995 and $10,000 a month and your Coach will dedicate a minimum of 5 hours a month to working with you on your sales, marketing, team building, business development, and every step of the *Action* Plan you created from your Alignment Consultation.

Unlike most consultants, your *Action* Coach will do more than just show you what to do. She'll be with you when you need her most, as each idea takes shape, as each campaign is put into place, as you need the little pointers on making it happen, when you need someone to talk to, when you're faced with challenges and, most importantly, when you're just not sure what to do next. Your Coach will be there every step of the way.

5. Why at least 12 months?

If you've been in business for more than a few weeks, you've seen at least one or two so called "quick fixes."

Most Consultants seem to think they can solve all your problems in a few hours or a few days. At *Action* we believe that long-term success means not just scraping the surface and doing it for you. It means doing it with you, showing you how to do it, working alongside you, and creating the success together.

Over the 12 months, you'll work on different areas of your business, and month by month you'll not only see your goals become a reality, you'll gain both the confidence and the knowledge to make it happen again and again, even when your first 12 months of Coaching is over.

6. How can you be sure this will work in my industry and in my business?

Very simple. You see at *Action,* we're experts in the areas of sales, marketing, business development, business management, and team building just to name a few. With 328 different profit-building strategies, you'll soon see just how powerful these systems are.

You, on the other hand, are the expert in your business and together we can apply the *Action* systems to make your business fly.

Add to this the fact that within the *Action* Team at least one of our Coaches has either worked with, managed, worked in, or even owned a business that's the same or very similar to yours. Your *Action* Coach has the full resources of the entire *Action* team to call upon for every challenge you have. Imagine hundreds of experts ready to help you.

7. Won't this just mean more work?

Of course when you set the plan with your *Action* Coach, it'll all seem like a massive amount of work, but no one ever said attaining your goals would be easy.

In the first few months, it'll take some work to adjust, some work to get over the hump so to speak. The further you are into the program, the less and less work you'll have to do.

You will, however, be literally amazed at how focused you'll be and how much you'll get done. With focus, an *Action* Coach, and most importantly the *Action* Systems, you'll be achieving a whole lot more with the same or even less work.

8. How will I find the time?

Once again the first few months will be the toughest, not because of an extra amount of work, but because of the different work. In fact, your *Action* Coach will show you how to, on a day-to-day basis, get more work done with less effort.

In other words, after the first few months you'll find that you're not working more, just working differently. Then, depending on your goals from about month six onwards, you'll start to see the results of all your work, and if you choose to, you can start working less than ever before. Just remember, it's about changing what you do with your time, *not* putting in more time.

9. How much will I need to invest?

Nothing, if you look at it from the same perspective as we do. That's the difference between a cost and an investment. Everything you do with your *Action* Coach is a true investment in your future.

Not only will you create great results in your business, but you'll end up with both an entrepreneurial education second to none, and the knowledge that you can repeat your successes over and over again.

As mentioned, you'll need to invest at least $1295 up to $5000 for the Alignment Consultation and Training Day, and then between $995 and $10,000 a month for the next 12 months of coaching.

Your Coach may also suggest several books, tapes, and videos to assist in your training, and yes, they'll add to your investment as you go. Why? Because having an *Action* Coach is just like having a marketing manager, a sales team leader, a trainer, a recruitment specialist, and corporate consultant all for half the price of a secretary.

10. Will it cost me extra to implement the strategies?

Once again, give your *Action* Coach just half an hour and he'll show you how to turn your marketing into an investment that yields sales and profits rather than just running up your expenses.

In most cases we'll actually save you money when we find the areas that aren't working for you. But yes, I'm sure you'll need to spend some money to make some money.

Yet, when you follow our simple testing and measuring systems, you'll never risk more than a few dollars on each campaign, and when we find the ones that work, we make sure you keep profiting from them time and again.

Remember, when you go the accounting way of saving costs, you can only ever add a few percent to the bottom line.

Following Brad Sugars' formula, your *Action* Coach will show you that through sales, marketing, and income growth, your possible returns are exponential.

The sky's the limit, as they say.

11. Are there any guarantees?

To put it bluntly, no. Your *Action* Coach will never promise any specific results, nor will she guarantee that any of your goals will become a reality.

You see, we're your coach. You're still the player, and it's up to you to take the field. Your Coach will push you, cajole you, help you, be there for you, and even do some things with you, but you've still got to do the work.

Only *you* can ever be truly accountable for your own success and at *Action* we know this to be a fact. We guarantee to give you the best service we can, to answer your questions promptly, and with the best available information. And, last but not least your *Action* Coach is committed to making you successful whether you like it or not.

That's right, once we've set the goals and made the plan, we'll do whatever it takes to make sure you reach for that goal and strive with all your might to achieve all that you desire.

Of course we'll be sure to keep you as balanced in your life as we can. We'll make sure you never compromise either the long-term health and success of your company or yourself, and more importantly your personal set of values and what's important to you.

12. What results have other business owners seen?

Anything from previously working 60 hours a week down to working just 10—right through to increases in revenues of 100s and even 1000s of percent. Results speak for themselves. Be sure to keep reading for specific examples of real people, with real businesses, getting real results.

There are three reasons why this will work for you in your business. Firstly, your *Action* Coach will help you get 100 percent focused on your goals and the step-by-step processes to get you there. This focus alone is amazing in its effect on you and your business results.

Secondly, your coach will hold you accountable to get things done, not just for the day-to-day running of the business, but for the dynamic growth of the business. You're investing in your success and we're going to get you there.

Thirdly, your Coach is going to teach you one-on-one as many of *Action's* 328 profit-building strategies as you need. So whether your goal is to be making more money, or working fewer hours or both inside the next 12 months your goals can become a reality. Just ask any of the thousands of existing *Action* clients, or more specifically, check out the results of 19 of our most recent clients shown later in this section.

13. What areas will you coach me in?

There are five main areas your *Action* Coach will work on with you. Of course, how much of each depends on you, your business, and your goals.

Sales. The backbone of creating a superprofitable business, and one area we'll help you get spectacular results in.

Marketing and Advertising. If you want to get a sale, you've got to get a prospect. Over the next 12 months your *Action* Coach will teach you Brad Sugars' amazingly simple streetwise marketing—marketing that makes profits.

Team Building and Recruitment. You'll never *wish* for the right people again. You'll have motivated and passionate team members when your Coach shows you how.

Systems and Business Development. Stop the business from running you and start running your business. Your Coach will show you the secrets to having the business work, even when you're not there.

Customer Service. How to deliver consistently, make it easy to buy, and leave your customers feeling delighted with your service. Both referrals and repeat business are centered in the strategies your Coach will teach you.

14. Can you also train my people?

Yes. We believe that training your people is almost as important as coaching you.

Your investment starts at $1500 for your entire team, and you can decide between five very powerful in-house training programs. From "*Sales Made Simple*" for your face-to-face sales team to "*Phone Power*" for your entire team's telephone etiquette and sales ability. Then you can run the *"Raving Fans"* customer service training or the *"Total Team"* training. And finally, if you're too busy earning a living to make any real money, then you've just got to attend our *"Business Academy 101."* It will make a huge impact on your finances, business, career, family, and lifestyle. You'll be amazed at how much involvement and excitement comes out of your team with each training program.

15. Can you write ads, letters, and marketing pieces for me?

Yes. Your *Action* Coach can do it for you, he can train you to do it yourself, or we can simply critique the marketing pieces you're using right now.

If you want us to do it for you, our one-time fees start at just $1195. You'll not only get one piece; we'll design several pieces for you to take to the market and see which one performs the best. Then, if it's a critique you're after, just $349 means we'll work through your entire piece and give you feedback on what to change, how to change it, and what else you should do. Last but not least, for between $15 and $795 we can recommend a variety of books, tapes, and most importantly, Brad Sugars' Instant Success series books that'll take you step-by-step through the how-tos of creating your marketing pieces.

16. Why do you also recommend books, tapes, and videos?

Basically, to save you time and money. Take Brad Sugars' *Sales Rich* DVD or Video Series, for instance. In about 16 hours you'll learn more about business than you have in the last 12 years. It'll also mean your *Action* Coach works with you on the high-level implementation rather than the very basic teaching.

It's a very powerful way for you to speed up the coaching process and get phenomenal rather than just great results.

17. When is the best time to get started?

Yesterday. OK, seriously, right now, today, this minute, before you take another step, waste another dollar, lose another sale, work too many more hours, miss another family event, forget another special occasion.

Far too many business people wait and see. They think working harder will make it all better. Remember, what you know got you to where you are. To get to where you want to go, you've got to make some changes and most probably learn something new.

There's no time like the present to get started on your dreams and goals.

18. So how do we get started?

Well, you'd better get back in touch with your *Action* Coach. There's some very simple paperwork to sign, and then you're on your way.

You'll have to invest a few hours showing them everything about your business. Together you'll get a plan created and then the work starts. Remember, it may seem like a big job at the start, but with a Coach, you're sharing the load and together you'll achieve great things.

Here's what others say about what happened after working with an *Action* business coach

Paul and Rosemary Rose—Icontact Multimedia

"Our *Action* coach showed us several ways to help market our product. We went on to triple our client base and simultaneously tripled our profits in just seven months. It was unbelievable! Last year was our best Christmas ever. We were really able to spoil ourselves!"

S. Ford—Pride Kitchens

"In 6 months, I've gone from working more than 60 hours per week in my business to less than 20, and my conversion rate's up from 19 percent to 62 percent. I've now got some life back!"

Gary and Leanne Paper—Galea Timber Products

"We achieved our goal for the 12 months within a 6-month period with a 100 percent increase in turnover and a good increase in margins. We have already recommended and will continue to recommend this program to others."

Russell, Kevin, John, and Karen—Northern Lights Power and Distribution

"Our profit margin has increased from 8 percent to 21 percent in the last 8 months. *Action* coaching focussed us on what are our most profitable markets."

Ty Pedersen—De Vries Marketing Sydney

"After just three months of coaching, my sales team's conversion rate has grown from an average of less than 12 percent to more than 23 percent and our profits have climbed by more than 30 percent."

Hank Meerkerk and Hemi McGarvey—B.O.P. School of Welding

"Last year we started off with a profit forecast, but as soon as we got *Action* involved we decided to double our forecast. We're already well over that forecast again by two-and-a-half times on turnover, and profits are even higher. Now we run a really profitable business."

Stuart Birch—Education Personnel Limited

"One direct mail letter added $40,000 to my bottom line, and working with *Action* has given me quality time to work on my business and spend time with my family."

Mark West—Wests Pumping and Irrigation

"In four months two simple strategies have increased our business more than 20 percent. We're so busy, we've had to delay expanding the business while we catch up!"

Michael Griffiths—Gym Owner

"I went from working 70 hours per week *in* the business to just 25 hours, with the rest of the time spent working *on* the business."

Cheryl Standring—In Harmony Landscapes

"We tried our own direct mail and only got a 1 percent response. With *Action* our response rate increased to 20 percent. It's definitely worth every dollar we've invested."

Jason and Chris Houston—Empradoor Finishing

"After 11 months of working with *Action,* we have increased our sales by 497 percent, and the team is working without our having to be there."

Michael Avery—Coomera Pet Motels

"I was skeptical at first, but I knew we needed major changes in our business. In 2 months, our extra profits were easily covering our investment and our predictions for the next 10 months are amazing."

Garry Norris—North Tax & Accounting

"As an accountant, my training enables me to help other business people make more money. It is therefore refreshing when someone else can help me do the same. I have a policy of only referring my clients to people who are professional, good at what they do, and who have personally given me great service. *Action* fits all three of these criteria, and I recommend *Action* to my business clients who want to grow and develop their businesses further."

Lisa Davis and Steve Groves—Mt. Eden Motorcycles

"With *Action* we increased our database from 800 to 1200 in 3 months. We consistently get about 20 new qualified people on our database each week for less than $10 per week."

Christine Pryor—U-Name-It Embroidery

"Sales for August this year have increased 352 percent. We're now targeting a different market and we're a lot more confident about what we're doing."

Joseph Saitta and Michelle Fisher—Banyule Electrics

"Working with *Action,* our inquiry rate has doubled. In four months our business has changed so much our customers love us. It's a better place for people to work and our margins are widening."

Kevin and Alison Snook—Property Sales

"In the 12 months previous to working with *Action,* we had sold one home in our subdivision. In the first eight months of working with *Action,* we sold six homes. The results speak for themselves."

Wayne Manson—Hospital Supplies

"When I first looked at the Mentoring Program it looked expensive, but from the inside looking out, its been the best money I have ever spent. Sales are up more than $3000 per month since I started, and the things I have learned and expect to learn will ensure that I will enjoy strong sustainable growth in the future."

◼ ActionCOACH Contact Details

ActionCOACH Global Office

5781 S. Fort Apache Road, Las Vegas, NV 89148

Ph: +1 (702) 795 3188

Fax: +1 (702) 795 3183

Free Call: (888) 483 2828

ActionCOACH Offices around the globe:

Australia | Brazil | Canada | China | Dominican Republic | England

France | Germany | Hong Kong | India | Indonesia | Ireland | Malaysia

Mexico | New Zealand | Nigeria | Phillippines | Portugal | Puerto Rico

Scotland | Singapore | S. Africa | Spain | Taiwan | USA | Wales

Here's how you can profit from all of Brad's ideas with your local ActionCOACH Business Coach

Just like a sporting coach pushes an athlete to achieve optimum performance, provides them with support when they are exhausted, and teaches the athlete to execute plays that the competition does not anticipate.

A business coach will make you run more laps than you feel like. A business coach will show it like it is. And a business coach will listen.

The role of an **ActionCOACH** Business Coach is to show you how to improve your business through guidance, support, and encouragement. Your coach will help you with your sales, marketing, management, team building, and so much more. Just like a sporting coach, your **ActionCOACH** Business Coach will help you and your business perform at levels you never thought possible.

Whether you've been in business for a week or 20 years, it's the right time to meet with and see how you'll profit from an **ActionCOACH.**

As the owner of a business it's hard enough to keep pace with all the changes and innovations going on in your industry, let alone to find the time to devote to sales, marketing, systems, planning and team management, and then to run your business as well.

As the world of business moves faster and becomes more competitive, having a Business Coach is no longer a luxury; it has become a necessity. Based on the sales, marketing, and business management systems created by Brad Sugars, your **ActionCOACH** is trained to not only show you how to increase your business revenues and profits but also how to develop your business so that you, as the owner, can take back control. All with the aim of your working less and relaxing more. Making money is one thing; having the time to enjoy it is another.

Your **ActionCOACH** Business Coach will become your marketing manager, your sales director, your training coordinator, your confidant, your mentor. In short, your **ActionCOACH** will help you make your business dreams come true.

ATTENTION BUSINESS OWNERS
You can increase your profits now

Here's how you can have one of Brad's **ActionCOACH** Business Coaches guide you to success.

Like every successful sporting icon or team, a business needs a coach to help it achieve its full potential. In order to guarantee your business success, you can have one of Brad's team as your business coach. You will learn about how you can get amazing results with the help of the team at **ActionCOACH.**

The business coaches are ready to take you and your business on a journey that will reward you for the rest of your life. You see, we believe **Action** speaks louder than words.

Complete and post this card to your local **ActionCOACH** office to discover how our team can help you increase your income today!

ActionCOACH

The World's Number 1 Business Coaching Firm

Name ....

Position ....

Company ....

Address ....

....

Country ....

Phone ....

Fax ....

Email ....

Referred by ....

How do I become an ActionCOACH Business Coach?

If you choose to invest your time and money in a great business and you're looking for a white-collar franchise opportunity to build yourself a lifestyle, an income, a way to take control of your life and, a way to get great personal satisfaction …

Then you've just found the world's best team!

Now, it's about finding out if you've got what it takes to really enjoy and thrive in this amazing business opportunity.

Here are the 4 things we look for in every ActionCOACH:

1. You've got to love succeeding

We're looking for people who love success, who love getting out there and making things happen. People who enjoy mixing with other people, people who thrive on learning and growing, and people who want to charge an hourly rate most professionals only dream of.

2. You've got to love being in charge of your own life

When you're ready to take control, the key is to be in business for yourself, but not by yourself. **ActionCOACH**'s support, our training, our world leading systems, and the backup of a global team are all waiting to give you the best chance of being an amazing business success.

3. You've got to love helping people

Being a great Coach is all about helping yourself by helping others. The first time clients thank you for showing them step by step how to make more money and work less within their business, will be the day you realize just how great being an **ActionCOACH** Business Coach really is.

4. You've got to love a great lifestyle

Working from home, setting your own timetable, spending time with family and friends, knowing that the hard work you do is for your own company and, not having to climb a so-called corporate ladder. This is what lifestyle is all about. Remember, business is supposed to give you a life, not take it away.

Our business is booming and we're seriously looking for people ready to find out more about how becoming a member of the **ActionCOACH** Business Coaching team is going to be the best decision you've ever made.

Apply online now at www.actioncoach.com

Here's how you can network, get new leads, build yourself an instant sales team, learn, grow and build a great team of supportive business owners around you by checking into your local ActionCOACH Profit Club

Joining your local ActionCOACH Profit Club is about more than just networking, it's also the learning and exchanging of profitable ideas.

Embark on a journey to a more profitable enterprise by meeting with fellow, like-minded business owners.

An **ActionCOACH** Profit Club is an excellent way to network with business people and business owners. You will meet every two weeks for breakfast to network and learn profitable strategies to grow your business.

Here are three reasons why **ActionCOACH** Profit Clubs work where other networking groups don't:

1. You know networking is a great idea. The challenge is finding the time and maintaining the motivation to keep it up and make it a part of your business. If you're not really having fun and getting the benefits, you'll find it gets easier to find excuses that stop you going. So, we guarantee you will always have fun and learn a lot from your bi-weekly group meetings.
2. The real problem is that so few people do any work 'on' their business. Instead they generally work "in" it, until it's too late. By being a member of an **ActionCOACH** Profit Club, you get to attend FREE business-building workshops run by Business Coaches that teach you how to work "on" your business and avoid this common pitfall and help you to grow your business.
3. Unlike other groups, we have marketing systems to assist in your groups' growth rather than just relying on you to bring in new members. This way you can concentrate on YOUR business rather than on ours.

Latest statistics show that the average person knows at least 200 other contacts. By being a member of your local **ActionCOACH** Profit Club, you have an instant network of around 3,000 people.

Join your local ActionCOACH Profit Club today.

Apply online now at www.actionprofitclub.com

LEVERAGE—The Game of Business
Your Business Success is just a Few Games Away

Leverage—The Game of Business is a fun way to learn how to succeed in business fast.

The rewards start flowing the moment you start playing!

Leverage is three hours of fun, learning, and discovering how you can be an amazingly successful business person.

It's a breakthrough in education that will have you racking up the profits in no time. The principles you take away from playing this game will set you up for a life of business success. It will open your mind to what's truly possible. Apply what you learn and **sit back and watch your profits soar.**

By playing this fun and interactive business game, you will learn:

- How to quickly raise your business income
- How business people can become rich and successful in a short space of time
- How to create a business that works without you

Isn't it time you had the edge over your competition?

Leverage has been played by all age groups from 12-85 and has been a huge learning experience for all. The most common comment we hear is: 'I thought I knew a lot, and just by playing a simple board game I have realized I have a long way to go. The knowledge I've gained from playing Leverage will make me thousands! Thanks for the lesson.'

To order your copy online today, please visit www.bradsugars.com